英汉对照·心灵阅读

Aspiration

励志篇

王亚男　编译
林　立　审校

外文出版社

卷首语

总有一种感动无处不在。

总有一种情怀轻舞飞扬。

总有一种生活，在别处，闪动异样的光芒。

阅读，让我们的生活在情调与知性中享受更多……

故事与见闻，犹如生活的魅力与智慧，合着我们自身生命的光与影，陪伴我们一路前行。

快乐和圆满，幻想与失落，飞扬的眼泪，

行走江湖的落拓，不与人说的痛苦，渐行渐远的繁华，坚持的勇气，点点滴滴的小意思……

人生让我们感受到的，也许远远不只是这些；更多的是挫折后生长的力量，沉闷时的豁然开朗，是屋前那静静的南山上盛开的人淡如菊的境界，是闹市中跋涉红尘、豪情万丈的冲动，是很纯粹的一杯午后的香醇的咖啡……

漫步红尘，有彻悟来自他人的故事，有灵犀来自偶然的相遇，在这里，一种从未见过的却可能早就在我们心底的生活方式有可能与我们邂逅。

让我们一起阅读吧，感受生长的智慧、风雅与力量。

Contents
目　录

Never give up

永不放弃

Trying times will pass,
As they always do.

难捱的时光终将过去，
一如既往。

Never give up,
Never lose hope.

Always have faith[1],
It allows you to cope.

Trying times will pass,
As they always do.

Just have patience[2],
Your dreams will come true.

So put on a smile,
You'll live through your pain.

Know it will pass,
And strength you will gain.

永不放弃，
永不心灰意冷。

永存信念，
它会使你应付自如。

难捱的时光终将过去，
一如既往。

只要有耐心，
梦想就会成真。

露出微笑，
你会走出痛苦。

相信苦难定会过去，
你将重获力量。

❶ **faith** /feɪθ/
n. 信念
❷ **patience** /ˈpeɪʃns/
n. 耐心

What you see is what you get

你得到的是你想到的

If you looked at a tree long enough, it will move.

如果你一直盯着一棵树看，树都会走路。

You've heard the expression, "What you see is what you get." My grandfather used to say: "If you looked at a tree long enough, it will move." We see what we want to see. Psychologists[1] tell us that nothing controls our lives more than our self-image[2]. We live like the person we see in the mirror. We are what we think we are. If you don't think you'll be successful, you won't. You can't be it if you can't see it. Your life is limited to your vision. If you want to change your life, you must change your vision of your life.

Arnold Schwarzenegger was not that famous in 1976 when he met with a newspaper reporter. The reporter asked Schwarzenegger: "Now that you've retired from bodybuilding[3], what do you plan to do next? Schwarzenegger answered very calmly and confidently: "I'm going to be the #1 movie star in Hollywood."The reporter was shocked and amused at Schwarzenegger's plan. At that time, it was very hard to imagine[4] how this muscle-bound[5] bodybuilder, who was not a professional actor and who spoke poor English with an strong Austrian accent, could ever hope to be Hollywood's #1 movie star!

So the reporter asked Schwarzenegger how he planned to make his dream come true, Schwarzenneger said: "I'll do it the same way I became the #1 bodybuilder in the world. What I do was to create a vision of who I want to be, then I start living like that person in my mind as if it were already true." Sounds almost childishly simple, doesn't it? But it worked! Schwarzenegger DID become the #1 highest paid movie star in Hollywood! Re-

你一定听过这样的说法："你得到的是你想到的"。我爷爷常常说："如果你一直盯着一棵树看，树都会走路。"我们看在眼里的是我们想要看的东西。心理学家告诉我们，比任何东西更能控制我们人生的是我们的自我意象。我们像在镜子里看到的自己一样地活着。自己是自我感觉的自己。如果你不认为自己会成功，那你就不会成功。你看不到也就达不到。你的人生是受你的抱负限制的。如果你想改变你的人生，你就必须改变你的人生理想。

阿诺·施瓦辛格在1976年遇见一位报社记者的时候还不太有名。那位记者问施瓦辛格："你现在从健美这一行退休下来，下一步准备做什么？"施瓦辛格平静自信地回答："我将成为好莱坞一流的电影明星"。那位记者为施瓦辛格的计划感到惊讶、可笑。在当时，人们很难想象这位肌肉结实的健美运动员，既非职业演员而且奥地利口音很重、英语很差，怎么可能成为好莱坞的一流明星?!

当那位记者问施瓦辛格怎样计划使梦想成真，施瓦辛格答道："我会照着使我成为世界一流的健美运动员的方法去做。我先设想出自己想成为的那个人，然后按照我心里想象的那个人去生活。"乍听起来是不是单纯得

❶ **psychologist**
/saɪˈkɒlədʒɪst/
n. 心理学家，心理学研究者

❷ **self-image**
n. 自我意象

❸ **bodybuilding**
/ˈbɒdɪˈbjuːdɪŋ/
n. （通过锻炼）增强体质

❹ **imagine**
/ɪˈmædʒɪn/
v. 想象，设想，预料

❺ **muscle-bound**
/ˈmʌslˈbaʊnd/
adj. （因锻炼过渡）肌肉粗而硬的

member: "If you can see it, you can be it."

A successful businessman I know wears a shirt with these words on it: "Don't just pursue your dreams. Chase 'em down and tackle[6] 'em!" You only get one life to live, so why not live the best life possible? So you can be fully satisfied at what you see and get. Just think a minute!

像孩子的话？但事实证明这样做的确成功了！施瓦辛格真的成了好莱坞收入第一的电影明星！记住：“如果你能想得到，你就能做得到”。

我认识一位很成功的商人，他穿着的T恤衫印着这样的话：“不要只追逐你的梦，要抓住它，征服它！”人生只有一次，为什么不过得最精彩呢？那样的话你就可以为你所想到的和所得到的感到满足。好好想想吧！

❻ **tackle** /ˈtækl/ *v.* 应付，处理，对付

If I were a boy again

如果我再次成为一个孩子

Inner sunshine warms not only the heart of the owner, but of all that come in contact with it.

内心的阳光不仅能够温暖自己的心，而且能够温暖周围人的心。

If I were a boy again, I would practice perseverance[1] oftener, and never give up a thing because it was hard or inconvenient. If we want light, we must conquer darkness. Perseverance can sometimes equal genius in its results. "There are only two creatures," says a proverb, "who can surmount[2] the pyramids — the eagle and the snail."

If I were a boy again, I would school myself into a habit of attention; I would let nothing come between the subject and me in hand. I would remember that a good skater never tries to skate in two directions at once. The habit of attention becomes part of our life, if we begin early enough. I often hear grown-up people say, "I could not fix my attention on the lecture or book, although I wished to do so," and the reason is, the habit was not formed in youth.

If I were to live my life over again, I would pay more attention to the cultivation of the memory. I would strengthen that faculty[3] by every possible means, and on every possible occasion. It takes a little hard work at first to remember things accurately; but memory soon helps itself, and gives very little trouble. It only needs early cultivation to become a power.

If I were a boy again, I would look on the cheerful side. Life is very much like a mirror: if you smile upon it, it smiles back upon you; but if you frown and look doubtful on it, you will get a similar look in return.

如果我能再当一回孩子的话，我会更经常地培养自己坚持不懈的精神，并且决不因其困难或者不方便而放弃一件事。如果我们想要光亮，我们必须战胜黑暗。坚持不懈的精神有时就相当于天分。一条谚语说："只有两种生物可以征服金字塔——鹰和蜗牛。"

如果我能再当一回孩子的话，我会使自己养成集中精神的习惯，我不让任何事情站在我和需要解决的事情中间。我会记住一个好的滑冰选手绝不会试图同时滑向两个方向。如果我们很早就开始培养的话，集中精神的习惯就会成为我们生活的一部分。我经常听一些成年人说："我不能集中精力听讲或看书，尽管我也希望这么做。"原因就是小时候没有养成这个习惯。

如果我能够重新生活一次的话，我会更加注意培养自己的记忆力。我会用任何可能的办法，在任何可能的场合加强这种能力。起初准确记住事物是有些困难，但记忆力很快会帮助它自己，并且也不那么费劲了。这只需要早期培养从而使之成为一种能力。

如果我能再当一回孩子的话，我会看到事物好的一面。生活很像一面镜子：如果你对它笑，它也对你笑；但是如果你对它皱眉头或疑惑地看着它，你也会得到一个相似的

❶ **perseverance**
/ˌpɜːsɪˈvɪərəns/
n. 坚持不懈，不屈不挠

❷ **surmount**
/səˈmaʊnt/
vt. 克服（困难等），处于或置于（某高物）的顶端

❸ **faculty**
/ˈfæklti/
n. 才能，本领，能力

Inner sunshine warms not only the heart of the owner, but of all that come in contact with it. "Who shuts love out, in turn shall be shut from love."

If I were a boy again, I would demand of myself more courtesy[4] towards my companions[5] and friends, and indeed towards strangers as well. The smallest courtesies along the rough roads of life are like the little birds that sing to us all winter long, and make that season of ice and snow more endurable[6].

Finally, instead of trying hard to be happy, as if that were the sole purpose of life, I would, if I were a boy again, try still harder to make others happy.

回应。

内心的阳光不仅能够温暖自己的心，而且能够温暖周围人的心。“拒绝爱的人，同时也会被爱拒绝。”

如果我能再当一回孩子的话，我会要求自己对伙伴、朋友更有礼貌一些，实际上对陌生人也一样。在不平坦的生活路上，小小的礼貌就如同整个冬天都对我们歌唱的小鸟，使那个冰雪的季节变得更加容易度过。

最后，不要总是刻意地使自己快乐，好像这就是我们生活的唯一目标，如果我再次成为一个孩子的话，我会更加努力，让其他人开心快乐。

❹ **courtesy**
/ˈkɜːtəsɪ/
n. 礼貌，客气

❺ **companion**
/kəmˈpænɪən/
n. 伙伴，同伴

❻ **endurable**
/ɪnˈdjurəbl/
adj. 可忍耐的，可容忍的

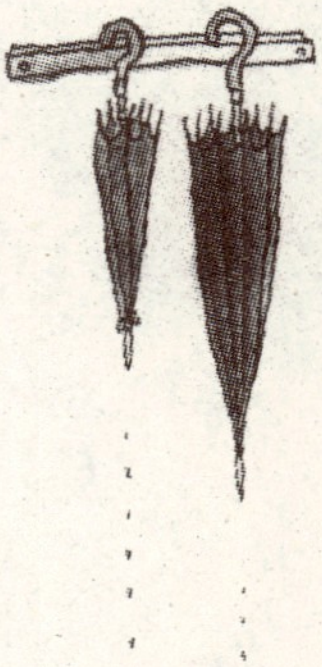

Do you accept challenges?

你接受挑战吗?

If we view our lives as a juggling act or a sort of sporting contest, we learn to go along with the limitations and obstacles that are dealt us.

如果我们把生活看作耍把戏或一种体育竞赛，我们就会学着赞同那些对我们的限制和阻碍。

Should we easily wail about[1] the embarrassment and the unfairness of life? Or should we accept obstacles as challenges? With a choice of stance[2] we can allow ourselves to be oppressed[3] victims. When anything happens to us, we can take it as a sign that we should not expect anything good out of our lives. These are times when we need to determine whether it is wisdom or fear that motivates us in our choices.

If we view our lives as a juggling[4] act or a sort of sporting contest, we learn to go along with the limitations and obstacles that are dealt us. We then find ways to make it through the event in good shape and with energy. Different talents and strengths will be called upon to get through the obstacles. Our faith, humor, and hope may be tested, but they are what keeps us going as we try to overcome the various obstacles.

Discrimination[5] and prejudice[6] are challenges. We force ourselves to work twice as hard as others; however, the rewards from our work are ours to enjoy. The important thing is to be working at something we find meaningful and worthwhile.

To succeed, you must accept challenges. There will always be barriers, cultural differences, and lack of understanding around us, but it is beneficial for us to stay together, be sensitive to each other needs, and to help each other. Maintaining cultural diversity and integrity[7] is possible as a healthy community builds on teamwork, praise, pride and enthusiasm. Once, we are dedi cated to improve critical skills such as knowledge sharing, collab-

我们应该轻易地为生活中的困难和不公平痛苦吗？或者，我们应该把障碍当作挑战来接受？由于选择不同的立场，我们可以使自己成为被压迫的受害者。不管发生什么事情，我们都可以把它看作不会有什么好事发生的标志。很多时候，我们需要确定是智慧还是恐惧使我们做出选择。

如果我们把生活看作耍把戏或一种体育竞赛，我们就会学着赞同那些对我们的限制和阻碍。然后我们就会寻找方法集中精力很好地解决这些问题。排除障碍需要不同的才能和力量。我们的信念、幽默感和希望都可能受到考验，但在我们试着克服各种各样的障碍时，它们使我们继续前行。

歧视和偏见是挑战。我们迫使自己比别人加倍努力工作；无论如何，工作的回报由我们自己来享用。重要的是做那些我们认为有意义、有价值的事情。

要成功，我们必须接受挑战。我们周围总会有障碍，文化差异以及缺乏了解，但对于我们来说团结是有益的，对彼此的需要应该敏感一些，而且互相帮助。对于一个建立在合作、奖励、自豪和热情基础上的健康集体而言，保持文化的差异与完整是可能的。一旦我们努力提高重要的技巧，如知识共享、

❶ **wail about**
痛苦，诉苦

❷ **stance**
/stæns/
n. 态度，观点，立场

❸ **oppressed**
/əˈpresd/
adj. 受压迫的，受压制的

❹ **juggle**
/ˈdʒʌgl/
v. 耍把戏

❺ **discrimination**
/dɪˌskrɪmɪˈneɪʃn/
n. 歧视

❻ **prejudice**
/ˈpredʒʊdɪs/
n. 偏见，成见

❼ **integrity**
/ɪnˈtegrətɪ/
n. 完整

oration[8], flexibility and risk taking, we will improve our future.

Together, we can make our world a better place in which to live by changing the way we and the rest of the population view it — positively. Let's make this challenge a reality.

合作、灵活性和冒险精神，我们就会改善我们的未来。

让我们一起通过改变我们和其他人的观点（变得更积极），来使我们生活的这个世界更美好吧。让我们把这个挑战变成现实。

❽ **collaboration**
/kəˌlæbəˈreɪʃn/
n. 合作，协作

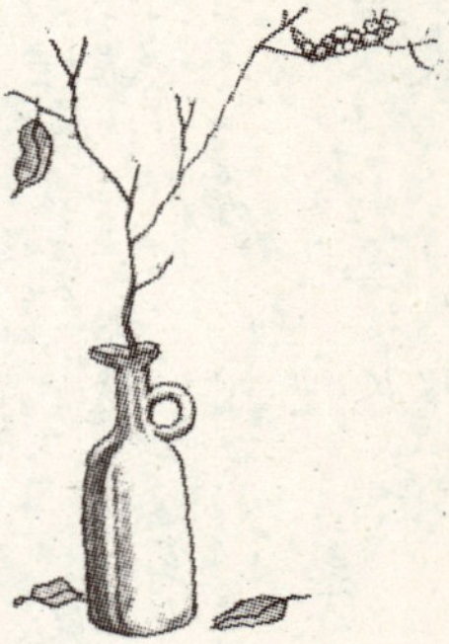

The principle of success

成功的准则

To live your life in your own way. To reach the goals you've set for yourself. To be the person you want to be.

按你自己的方式生活，达到你为自己定的目标，成为真实的自我。

What is success?

I am not going to try to define success. I think a precise definition is impossible. Is it winning a Gold Medal at the Olympic Games or winning Wimbledon, or being awarded a Nobel Prize[1]? What else? I believe personal success could be anything at all — it does not have to involve public recognition. Who is more successful? A millionaire who is unhappy, or an unnoticed person who has led a simple, happy life? The simplest definition of success I think is 'to set out to do something and to succeed in doing it'. It really doesn't matter what, or how humble the undertaking is.

Believe you can succeed and you will. Achieving success in whatever endeavor you choose may be the goal of life. Because it gives you freedom from worry. Could that be?

Success means different things to every one of us. Some people believe it is measured in financial terms, i.e. having wealth; others believe it is helping others rather than helping themselves. A bit of both perhaps! Or it could be simply achieving for achievement's sake. Success is such a personal thing. To many people it is the very root of their being — the reason for existing is to achieve something worthwhile in our lives. To the vast majority of the population it doesn't matter much whether they want to be successful or not; that's OK by me, as long as that is what you really want and you are happy with life. However, most people want and are motivated to a great extent[2] by public recognition

成功是什么？

我并不是要给成功下定义。我认为不可能有一个精确的定义。成功是在奥运会上赢得金牌吗？是赢得温布尔顿大奖吗？是获得诺贝尔奖吗？还是其他的什么？我认为个人的成功可以是任何事情——它不需要公众认可。谁更成功一些呢？是不快乐的亿万富翁还是过着简单、幸福生活的不引人注意的人？我认为成功最简单的定义是：开始做一件事情并且圆满地完成它。这件事情是什么，或是多么不起眼并不重要。

相信你可以成功你就会成功。努力达到你选择的成功也许是你生活的目标，因为它使你不再有任何担心，是那样吗？

成功的含义对于我们每个人来说都不同。一些人认为成功要靠钱的多少决定，比如，有财富；另一些人认为成功是帮助其他人而不是他们自己。也许两个都有一点儿！或者成功只是为了成功而已。成功是十分个性化的事情。对于许多人来说成功是他们生存的根本——存在就是为了完成我们生命中一些有价值的事情。对于大多数人来说，他们是否想成功并不重要；只要这是你想要的并且这样你可以快乐地生活，对于我本人无所谓。尽管如此，大多数人盼望并且有动力去追求

❶ **Nobel Prize**
诺贝尔奖

❷ **to a great extent**
在很大程度上

and a relentless[3] pursuit of achievement. How many people too are really happy? How many people are really doing what they want to with their lives? (Incidentally, the ability to imagine makes us different from animals).

No matter what motivates you personally...whatever you choose to do with your life, don't expect instant success. The years of struggle, commitment and learning in excelling at whatever endeavor[4] or trade you choose, is no easy task. I would wholeheartedly agree with that statement. It takes a lot of courage, character and discipline to achieve success in any field. Nearly all successful people have doubted themselves at some point and wanted to give up. Yet they carried on. So many people give up within an inch or two away from the gold in the seam[5] down the mine — a whisker away from success. One thing is for sure: success breeds SUCCESS, as it gathers a momentum[6] of its own and you get on a inning streak when everything seems to fit into place.

I like all of the following quotations[7]. They all stand for what success means to me personally. So I'll share them with you...

"Success is the continuous journey towards the achievement of predetermined worthwhile goals." "To live your life in your own way. To reach the goals you've set for yourself. To be the person you want to be — that is success."

公众在很大程度上的认可并且坚持不懈地追求有所成就。多少人是真正快乐的呢？多少人真的在做他们想做的事情？（补充一句，想象的能力使我们和动物有所区别。）

不管是什么鼓舞你，你一生选择做什么，都不要期待立刻成功。奋斗、努力、学习如何做好你选择的事情的日子并不那么容易过。我完全同意这种说法。在任何领域取得成就都需要勇气、品质和自律。几乎所有成功的人在某个时刻都曾怀疑过他们自己，并且想要放弃。但他们坚持下来了。许多人在距离矿井中的金矿层只有一两英寸时放弃了——差一点儿就成功了。有一件事可以肯定：成功培育成功，因为成功聚集了自己的动力；当每件事都顺利时，你可以连赢几局。

我喜欢所有下面这些话，它们都可以代表我个人所理解的成功的意义。我将与你分享这些话。

“成功是一段向着事先决定的、有价值的目标不断前进的旅程。”“按你自己的方式生活，达到你为自己定的目标，成为真实的自我——那就是成功。”

❸ **relentless** /rɪˈlentlɪs/ *adj.* 坚持不懈

❹ **endeavor** /ɪnˈdevə/ *n.* 努力，尽力

❺ **seam** /siːm/ *n.* 缝；矿层

❻ **momentum** /məˈmentəm/ *n.* 动力；势头

❼ **quotation** /kwəʊˈteɪʃn/ *n.* 引文

A lesson for living

生活的经验

If you carry on, one day something good will happen.

如果你坚持不懈，总有一天美好的事情会发生。

"Everything happens for the best," my mother said whenever I faced disappointment[1]. "If you carry on, one day something good will happen. And you'll realize that it wouldn't have happened if not for that previous disappointment."

Mother was right, as I discovered after graduating from college in 1932. I had decided to try for a job in radio, then work my way up to sports announcer. I hitchhiked[2] on the door of every station — and got turned down every time.

In one studio, a kind lady told me that big stations couldn't risk hiring an inexperienced person. "Go out in the sticks[3] and find a small station that'll give you a chance," she said.

I thumbed[4] home to Dixon, Ill. While there were no radio-announcing jobs in Dixon, my father said Montgomery Ward had opened a store and wanted a local athlete to manage its sports department. Since Dixon was where I had played high-school football, I applied. The job sounded just right for me. But I wasn't hired.

My disappointment must have shown. "Everything happens for the best," Mom reminded me.

Dad offered me the car to drive 70 miles to the Tri-Cities. I tried WOC Radio in Davenport, Iowa. The program director, a wonderful Scotsman named Peter Macarthur, told me they had already hired an announcer.

"每件事都会有个圆满的结局"，无论何时我面对失望，妈妈都会这么说。"如果你坚持不懈，总有一天美好的事情会发生，并且你会意识到如果没有以前的沮丧，美好的事就不会发生。"

1932 年我大学毕业后，发现妈妈是对的。我已经决定尝试找一家电台工作，然后逐步做到体育节目播音员。我搭便车到每个电台但是每次都被拒绝。

在一个播音室，一位好心的女士告诉我，大的电台不会冒险雇用一个没有经验的人。"出去到远离城市的边远地方，并找一个小的电台，那会给你一个机会。"她说。

我搭便车回到了家，伊利诺伊州的迪克森。当时在迪克森没有电台广播的工作，我父亲说蒙哥马利·沃德开了一家商店，并且需要一个当地的运动员管理体育用品部。因为迪克森是我高中打橄榄球的地方，我申请了那个职位。工作听起来对我很适合，但我没能被录用。

我的失望一定挂在了脸上。"每件事都会有个圆满的结局，"妈妈提醒我。

父亲提供给我一辆车，开出 70 里路到了 Tri-Cities。我试着去了爱荷华州达文波特的 WOC 电台。节目负责人是一个叫彼特·麦克

❶ **disappointment**
/ˌdɪsəˈpɔɪntmənt/
n. 失望，沮丧

❷ **hitchhike**
/ˈhɪtʃˈhaɪk/
v. 搭便车，要求(搭便车)

❸ **the sticks**
远离城市的边远地方

❹ **thumb**
/θʌm/
v. 向路过的机动车竖起拇指表示要求免费搭便车

As I left his office, my frustration[5] boiled over. I asked aloud, "How can a fellow get to be a sports announcer if he can't get a job in a radio station?" I was waiting for the elevator when I heard MacArthur calling, "What was that you said about sports? Do you know anything about football?" Then he stood me before a microphone and asked me to broadcast an imaginary game.

The preceding autumn, my team had won a game in the last 20 seconds with a 65-yard run. I did a 15-minute buildup to that play, and Peter told me I would be broadcasting Saturday's game!

On my way home, as I have many times since, I thought of my mother's words: "If you carry on, one day something good will happen — something that wouldn't have happened if not for that previous disappointment."

I often wonder what direction my life might have taken if I'd gotten the job at Montgomery Ward.

阿瑟的好心的苏格兰人，他告诉我他们已经雇用了一个广播员。

当我离开他的办公室时，我沮丧至极。我大声问“如果一个人在电台都不能找到工作，他又怎么能成为一个体育播音员呢？”这时我正在等电梯，我突然听到麦克阿瑟问，“你刚才说什么？体育？你知道关于足球的事吗？”然后他让我站在麦克风前播了一段想象的体育比赛。

前一个秋天，我们的球队以一个65码的跑动在最后20秒钟赢得了一场比赛。我对那场比赛作了一个15分钟的评论，然后彼得告诉我：我可以播星期六的节目。

在回家的路上，我又一次想起妈妈的话：“如果你坚持不懈，总有一天美好的事情会发生；如果没有以前的失望，美好的事就不会发生。”

我经常想如果我得到了蒙哥马利·沃德的工作，我的生命将转向哪个方向。

❺ **frustration** /frʌ'streɪʃn/ *n.* 灰心，沮丧

Freeman: Australian heroine

弗里曼：
澳大利亚的女英雄

What I love so much about life is that it's a mystery and who knows what lies ahead.

我为什么这么爱生活，就因为生活是个谜，谁也不知道前面有些什么。

At 16 years of age Freeman won gold at the Commonwealth Games as part of the 4×100m relay team. In 1990 she was awarded[1] Young Australian of the Year, and Aboriginal Athlete of the Year in 1991. In 1992 Freeman became the first Aboriginal track and field athlete to represent Australia at an Olympic Games. She became one of popular figures after winning the gold medal in the 400-meter-race at the Olympic Games 2000 held in her motherland.

It all started in Atlanta, that was the first time I saw her, I said to myself damn, she's kind a cute I must tune in tomorrow for a second glimpse[2]. The next time I saw her, she looked even better. After the Olympic Games I was somewhat obsessed[3] with seeing her again; mostly due to the fact that it was next to impossible to find anything on her, that little glimpse wasn't enough. Soon, I started looking for track magazines, books, and watching track shows every time they were aired, I didn't even like track, I just watched to see her run. Guess you can see Freeman was my introduction to track and field. With the track and field, I observed, I learned more about the sport and the major players involved in it.

Not only is Cathy Freeman good-looking and an athlete who possesses supreme[4] physical talents but also she's a great woman with a wonderful personality as well. She represents her Aborigine people to the fullest, fights for them, and gives them something to believe in. Cathy is a hero for Aborigines and non-Aborigines alike. In this day of sports when most athletes think of only themselves, Cathy is one of the few who makes a conscious

16岁时，弗里曼作为4×100m接力队的一员，在英联邦运动会上赢得了金牌。1990年，她被授予该年度澳大利亚杰出青年奖；1991年又获得该年度最佳土著运动员奖。1992年，弗里曼成为代表澳大利亚参加奥林匹克运动会的第一名土著田径运动员。获得了在自己祖国举办的2000年奥运会女子400米金牌后，她成了澳大利亚最受欢迎的人物之一。

一切都开始于亚特兰大。那是我第一次看见她。我对自己说，天呐，她太漂亮了，我明天一定要仔细看看她。我第二次看到她时，她更加漂亮了。奥运会结束后，我心中总想着要再见到她，主要是因为一切美好的东西都能在她身上找到，短短的一瞥是不够的。不久，我开始寻找竞赛运动的杂志、书籍，抓住每一次观看田径赛事转播的机会。我不大喜欢田径运动，我只是为了观看她赛跑的英姿。可以说是弗里曼领我步入田径之门。在田径运动里，我观察到和学到了许多有关这项运动的知识，也更多地了解了这项运动的主要选手。

卡西·弗里曼不仅美丽，是一位拥有超凡运动天分的运动员，而且也是一位具有优秀品格的伟大女性。她最完整地代表了土著民

❶ **award**
/əˈwɔːd/
vt. 颁发，授予

❷ **glimpse**
/ɡlɪmps/
n. 一瞥，一看

❸ **obsess**
/əbˈses/
vt. 使(某人)牵挂、惦念、着迷或困扰

❹ **supreme**
/suːˈpriːm/
adj. 最重要的，最大的，至高无上的

effort to represent herself as a positive role model. She's an extremely intelligent[5] young woman who knows who she is and is proud of it. Cathy is a very special person who can light up a whole room. Her beauty lies within as well as on the outside.

Now she's won the gold in the 400-meter-race at the Olympics. She is truly the best at her game. Not only does Cathy make her fellow Australians proud but many around the world. With the lighting of the torch at 2000 Olympic Games, Cathy brought Australians closer together.

When asked about her future after the race, guess how Cathy replied? "Every second my thoughts take me somewhere else. Retirement? Sure, it's crossed my mind. Living in another country? Sure, it's crossed my mind. What I love so much about life is that it's a mystery and who knows what lies ahead. My plan now is just to get a massage[6] right away."

族，为他们奋斗，给他们信心。卡西既是土著人的英雄，也是非土著人的英雄。在当今的运动届，多数运动员只为自己着想，卡西是自觉地以一种积极的角色展现自我的少数人物之一。她是一位聪明绝顶的年轻女子，懂得自身的价值并为此感到骄傲。卡西是一个能够照亮整间屋子的特殊的人。她的美丽不仅在于外表，也同样表现在内心。

现在她已赢得了400米赛的奥运会金牌。她在这项运动中是最棒的。她不仅使澳大利亚同胞感到骄傲，也使全世界许多人感到骄傲。随着2000年奥运会圣火的点燃，卡西将澳大利亚人更加紧密地连在了一起。

当比赛后被问及自己的将来时，猜猜卡西是怎样回答的？她说，“每分每秒我都有不同的想法。退役？当然闪过这种念头。到另一个国家定居？当然也曾想过。我为什么这么爱生活，就因为生活是个谜，谁也不知道前面有些什么。我现在的计划就是马上去做个按摩。”

❺ **intelligent**
/ɪnˈtelɪdʒənt/
adj. 聪明的，有才智的，有头脑的

❻ **massage**
/ˈmæsɑːʒ/
n. 按摩，推拿

Jessie's glove

杰西的手套

People remember more how much an employer cares than how much the employer pays.

人们记住更多的是雇主的关心，而不是他们所付的工资。

I do a lot of management training each year for the Circle K Corporation, a national chain of convenience stores[1]. Among the topics we address in our seminars is the retention[2] of quality employees — a real challenge to managers when you consider the pay scale[3] in the service industry. During these discussions, I ask the participants, "What has caused you to stay long enough to become a manager?" Some time back a new manager took the question and slowly, with her voice almost breaking, said, "It was a $19 baseball glove."

Cynthia told the group that she originally took a Circle K clerk job as an interim[4] position while she looked for something better. On her second or third day behind the counter[5], she received a phone call from her nine-year-old son, Jessie. He needed a baseball glove for Little League. She explained that as a single mother, money was very tight, and her first check would have to go for paying bills. Perhaps she could buy his baseball glove with her second or third check.

When Cynthia arrived for work the next morning, Patricia, the store manager, asked her to come to the small room in back of the store that served as an office. Cynthia wondered if she had done something wrong or left some part of her job incomplete from the day before. She was concerned and confused.

Patricia handed her a box. "I overheard[6] you talking to your son yesterday," she said, "and I know that it is hard to explain things to kids. This is a baseball glove for Jessie because he may not

我每年都为K循环公司做许多管理方面的培训，这是一家全国连锁的高质量高价的自助食品商店。在我们研讨会上发言的题目是留住高质量的雇员（在服务业当你考虑薪工标准时，这对管理者是个真正的挑战）。在讨论过程中，我问参与者："是什么使你们待得时间足够长从而成为管理者的?"过了一段时间，一个新的管理者接受了这个问题，声音中带着悲伤，慢慢地说："是一副19美元的棒球手套。"

辛西娅告诉这些人，她开始在K循环公司做的是临时办事员，当时她还在找一份更好的工作。在她第二或第三天站在柜台后时，她接到了她9岁儿子杰西的电话。他参加利特尔联盟需要一副棒球手套。她向他解释：作为一个单身妈妈，钱十分紧张，而且她的第一笔钱要用来付账。也许她第二次或第三次发钱可以给他买棒球手套。

当辛西娅第二天早晨来上班时，商店的管理者帕特丽夏让她到商店后面被当作办公室的小房间来一下。辛西娅想知道是不是前几天她做了什么错事或是没完成什么工作，她很担心也很迷惑。

帕特丽夏递给她一个盒子。"昨天我无意中听到了你和你儿子的谈话，"她说，"我

❶ **convenience stores**
[美]高质高价的自助食品商店
❷ **retention**
/rɪˈtenʃn/
n. 保持力
❸ **the pay scale**
薪工标准
❹ **interim**
/ˈɪntərɪm/
adj. 临时的，过渡时期，暂定
❺ **counter**
/ˈkaʊntə/
n. 柜台
❻ **overhear**
/ˌəʊvəˈhɪə/
v. 无意间听到

understand how important he is, even though you have to pay bills before you can buy gloves. You know we can't pay good people like you as much as we would like to; but we do care, and I want you to know you are important to us."

The thoughtfulness[7], empathy and love of this convenience store manager demonstrates vividly that people remember more how much an employer cares than how much the employer pays. An important lesson for the price of a Little League baseball glove.

知道很难向小孩子解释一些事情。这是给杰西的棒球手套，因为他可能不理解他对你是多么重要，尽管你必须先付帐才能给他买手套。你知道我们想给像你这样的优秀者很高的薪水，可做不到；但是我们的确在乎人才，我希望你知道你对我们十分重要。”

这个自助食品商店的管理者的体贴、关心和爱心，生动地证明了：人们记住更多的是雇主的关心，而不是他们所付的工资。一副利特尔棒球手套给我们上了重要的一课。

❼ **thoughtfulness**
/ˈθɔːtflnɪs/
n. 体贴

Still I rise

我仍奋起

You may trod me in the very dirt
But still, like dust, I' ll rise.

你可以把我踩进泥地
但像尘土，我仍将奋起。

You may write me down in history
With your bitter, twisted[1] lies,
You may trod me in the very dirt
But still, like dust, I'll rise.

Does my sassiness[2] upset you?
Why are you beset with gloom?
'Cause I walk like I've got oil wells
Pumping in my living room.

Just like moons and like suns,
With the certainty of tides,
Just like hopes springing high,
Still I'll rise.

Did you want to see me broken?
Bowed head and lowered eyes?
Shoulders falling down like teardrops,
Weakened by my soulful cries?

Does my haughtiness[3] offend you?
Don't you take it awful hard
'Cause I laugh like I've got gold mines
Diggin' in my own backyard.

You may shoot me with your words,
You may cut me with your eyes,

你可以把我写进历史
用你那尖刻的、撒谎的文字,
你可以把我踩进泥地
但像尘土,我仍将奋起。

我的精神抖擞可让你烦恼?
为什么你要皱着眉头?
因为我步履矫健
像家有油井滚滚流。

像月亮,像太阳,
浪潮退却亦复涨,
扬得高高像希望,
我仍将奋起。

你可曾想见到我颓丧?
俯首低头,目光低垂?
弯着腰身像落泪
弱不禁风,心在哭泣?

我的铮铮傲骨可让你厌恶?
别难受,别在乎
因为我笑声爽朗
像在自家后院采掘金矿。

你可以用言词向我射击,
你可以用目光向我砍劈,

❶ **twisted**
/ˈtwɪstɪd/
adj. 歪曲的
❷ **sassiness**
/ˈsæsɪnɪs/
n. 精神抖擞
❸ **haughtiness**
/ˈhɔːtɪnɪs/
n. 傲骨

You may kill me with your hatefulness,
But still, like air, I'll rise.

Does my sexiness upset you?
Does it come as a surprise
That I dance like I've got diamonds
At the meeting of my thighs[4]?

Out of the huts of history's shame
I rise
Up from a past that's rooted in pain
I rise
I'm a black ocean, leaping and wide,
Welling and swelling I bear in the tide.

Leaving behind nights of terror and fear
I rise
Into a daybreak that's wondrously clear
I rise
Bringing the gifts that my ancestors[5] gave,
I am the dream and the hope of the slave.
I rise
I rise
I rise.

你可以用仇恨将我击毙，
但像空气，我仍将奋起。

我的性感迷人可让你烦恼？
我的翩翩舞蹈可让你惊奇？
因为我舞姿飞扬
像我大腿交叉处拥有钻石。

从历史耻辱的茅舍
我奋起
从逝去的苦难岁月
我奋起
是黑色的海洋，水阔浪高
汹涌澎湃，领舵弄潮。

把恐怖的黑夜抛在身后
我奋起
走向光明灿烂的白昼
我奋起
带着祖先赐予的力量，
我是奴隶的梦想和希望
我奋起
我奋起
我奋起。

❹ **thigh** /θaɪ/
n. 大腿
❺ **ancestor**
/ˈænsestə/
n. 祖先

Life is to be whole

人生在于完整

We are more whole when we are missing something.

当我们失去某些东西时，我们反而感到更加完整。

Once a circle missed a wedge[1]. The circle wanted to be whole, so it went around looking for its missing piece. But because it was incomplete and therefore could roll[2] only very slowly, it admired the flowers along the way. It chatted with worms. It enjoyed the sunshine. It found lots of different pieces, but none of them fit. So it left them all by the side of the road and kept on searching. Then one day the circle found a piece that fit perfectly. It was so happy. Now it could be whole, with nothing missing. It incorporated[3] the missing piece into itself and began to roll. Now that it was a perfect circle, it could roll very fast, too fast to notice the flowers or talking to the worms. When it realized how different the world seemed when it rolled so quickly, it stopped, left its found piece by the side of the road and rolled slowly away.

The lesson of the story, I suggested, was that in some strange sense we are more whole when we are missing something. The man who will never know that it feels like to yearn[4], to hope, to nourish[5] his soul with the dream of something better. He will never know the experience of having someone who loves him give him something he has always wanted or never had.

There is a wholeness about the person who has come to terms with his limitations, who has been brave enough to let go of his unrealistic dreams and not feel like a failure for doing so. There is a wholeness about the man or woman who has learned that he or she is strong enough to go through a tragedy and survive[6]. Who can lose someone and still feel like a complete person.

从前有一只圆圈缺了一块楔子。圆圈想保持完整，于是四处寻找失去的那块楔子。但因为它不完整，因此只能滚动得很慢。它对路上遇到的花儿羡慕不已。它与蠕虫谈天说地。它欣赏着阳光的美丽。圆圈找到了许多不同的配件，但是没有一件与它相配的。所以，它把它们统统丢在路旁，继续寻觅。终于有一天，它找到了一个完美的配件。圆圈是那么的高兴。现在它是完整而没有缺憾的。它装好配件后滚动起来。既然它是一个完整的圆圈，它滚动得非常快，快得已无暇观赏花儿，也无暇与蠕虫倾诉心声。圆圈飞奔疾驰，发现眼中的世界如此的不同，它停下来，将找到的那个配件留在路旁，又开始了慢慢的滚动。

我觉得这个故事告诉我们，从某种奇妙的感觉上讲，当我们失去某些东西时，我们反而感到更加完整。一个人拥有一切其实在某些方面是个穷人。他永远体会不到什么是渴望、期待和对美好梦想的感悟。他永远不会有这种体验：一个爱他的人送给他那些他梦寐以求的或者是从未拥有过的东西意味着什么。

人生的完整在于一个人知道如何面对他的缺陷，如何勇敢地抛开那些不切实际的幻

❶ **wedge** /wedʒ/
n. 楔子
❷ **roll** /rəʊl/
vt. 滚动
❸ **incorporate** /ɪnˈkɔːpəreɪt/
v. 合并，将（某事物）作为整体的一部分
❹ **yearn** /jɜːn/
vi. 渴望
❺ **nourish** /ˈnʌrɪʃ/
vt. 滋养，（比喻）抱有，保持
❻ **survive** /səˈvaɪv/
v. 继续生存或存在

Life is not a trap set for us by God so that he can condemn[7] us for failing. Life is not a spelling bee, where no matter how many words you've gotten right, you're disqualified if you make one mistake. Life is more like a baseball season, where even the best team loses one-third of its games and even the worst team has its days of brilliance[8]. Our goal is to win more games than we lose.

When we accept that imperfection is part of being human, and when we can continue rolling through life and appreciate it, we will have achieved a wholeness that others can only aspire to. That, I believe, is what God asks of us — not "Be perfect", not "Don't even make a mistake", but "Be whole."

If we are brave enough to love, strong enough to forgive, generous enough to rejoice in another's happiness, and wise enough to know there is enough love to go around for us all, then we can achieve a fulfillment that no other living creature will ever know.

想而又不以此为缺憾。人生的完整性还在于一个男人或女人懂得：他（她）能够坚强地战胜人生的悲剧并继续生存，能够在失去亲人后依然表现出一个完整的人的风范。

人生不是上帝为谴责我们的缺陷而给我们布下的陷阱。人生不是一场拼字游戏，不管你拼出多少单词，一旦出现了一个错误就前功尽弃。人生更像一个棒球赛季，即使最好的球队整个比赛也会输掉1/3，而最差的球队也有风光的时候。

当我们接受了不完整性是人类本性的一部分，当我们继续滚动人生并欣赏人生，我们就会达到人生的完整，但对于别人来讲只能是个梦想。我相信上帝对我们的要求是：不求“完美”，不求“永不犯错误”，而求“完整”。

如果我们能够勇敢地去爱，能够坚强地去宽容，能够大度地分享别人的幸福，明智地理解在我们的身边充满爱，那么我们就能取得别的生物所不能取得的成就。

❼ **condemn**
/kən'dem/
vt. 谴责，责备

❽ **brilliance**
/'brɪlɪənt/
n. 光辉夺目，才华横溢

My heart goes out to you

我很同情你

The human spirit can be an amazing thing, and sometimes you encounter it at its very best when you aren't even looking.

人们的精神是十分令人惊异的事物，有时甚至当你自己都没注意时，你发现它处于最佳状态。

Sometimes you find the human spirit at its very best when you aren't even looking.

Douglas Maurer, 15, of Creve Coeur, Mo., had been feeling bad for days. His temperature ranged between 103 and 105 degrees, and he had severe flu-like symptoms. Finally his mother, Donna, took him to Children's Hospital at Washington University Medical Center in St. Louis. Blood tests revealed leukemia[1].

During the next 48 hours, Douglas endured blood transfusions, spinal and bone marrow tests and chemotherapy[2]. He developed pneumonia[3]. For ten days his mother stayed in his hospital room. One night Douglas, afraid, asked her to sleep in his bed by his side. Through her tears, she had to tell him she couldn't; I.V. tubes were attached to his body, the bed was small, and there was no room.

The doctors were frank, telling Douglas that for the next three years he would have to undergo chemotherapy. He would go bald and probably gain weight. Learning this, Douglas became even more discouraged; although he was told that there was a good chance of remission[4], he was smart enough to know that leukemia can be fatal.

On the day Douglas was admitted, his first time in a hospital, he had opened his eyes, looked around his room and said to his mother, "I thought you get flowers when you're in the hospital." Hearing this, an aunt called Brix Florist in St. Louis to order an ar-

有时，甚至当你不注意时，你会发现人的精神处于最佳状态。

密苏里州的道格拉斯·莫勒，15 岁，这些天一直身体不舒服。他的体温到了 103 至 105 华氏度，并有严重的类似感冒的症状。最后他的妈妈唐娜把他带到了圣路易斯华盛顿大学医学中心的儿童医院。验血的结果是他患了白血病。

接下来的 48 小时，道格拉斯经受了输血、骨髓检查和化学疗法。他又得了肺炎。十天以来他妈妈一直呆在医院的病房里。一天晚上，道格拉斯怕妈妈累坏了，让妈妈在身边睡一觉。她用眼泪告诉他，她不能；I.V.管子连在他的身体上，床很小，没有地方。

医生很直率地告诉道格拉斯，以后的三年他必须忍受化疗。他的头会变秃，体重可能也会增加。知道这些后，道格拉斯变得更灰心了。尽管人们告诉他病痛会减轻，但聪明的他知道白血病是致命的。

一天道格拉斯住院了，这是他第一次住院，他睁开眼，看了看病房，对他妈妈说："我认为住院的时候会有人送花。"听到这句话，一位姨妈打电话向圣路易斯的布里克斯花店订花。售货员的声音很高，听起来挺年轻的。姨妈觉得一个没经验的职员可能不知

❶ **leukemia** /luːˈkiːmɪə/ *n.* 白血病

❷ **chemotherapy** /ˌkiːməʊˈθerəpɪ/ *n.* 化学疗法

❸ **pneumonia** /njuːˈməʊnɪə/ *n.* 肺炎

❹ **remission** /rɪˈmɪʃn/ *n.* （病痛等的）缓解，减轻

rangement. The voice of the salesclerk was highpitched[5], and she sounded young. The aunt imagined an inexperienced clerk who would be unaware of the arrangement's significance.

So the aunt said, "I want the planter especially attractive. It's for my teen-age nephew who has leukemia."

"Oh," said the salesclerk. "Let's add some fresh-cut flowers to brighten it up."

When the arrangement arrived at the hospital, Douglas was feeling strong enough to sit up; he opened the envelope and read the card from his aunt.

Then he saw another card. His mother said it must have been meant for another arrangement. Douglas removed it anyway. The card said:

Douglas — I took your order. I work at Brix Florist. I had leukemia when I was seven years old. I'm 22 years old now. Good luck. My heart goes out to you. Sincerely, Laura Bradley.

Douglas's face lighted up. For the first time since he entered the hospital, he had been inspired. He had talked to so many doctors and nurses. But this one card was the thing that made him believe he might beat the disease[6].

I called Brix Florist and asked to speak with Laura Bradley.

道订花的重要意义。

所以姨妈说："我希望花能特别迷人。它是给我十几岁得了白血病的侄子的。"

"噢。"售货员说。"让我们加一些新摘的花使它更漂亮吧。"

当订的花送到医院时，道格拉斯有劲坐起来了，他打开信封看姨妈给他的贺卡。

然后他看到了另一张贺卡。他妈妈说这肯定是下次订花用的。不管怎么样道格拉斯打开了。卡上写着：

道格拉斯——你的花是在我这里订的。我在布里克斯花店工作。我7岁时得了白血病，现在我22岁了。祝你好运！我同情你。真诚的朋友，劳拉·布拉德利。

道格拉斯容光焕发。自从进了医院，他第一次感到鼓舞。他和许多医生和护士交谈过。但是这张贺卡使他相信他能够战胜疾病。

我打电话给布里克斯花店，要求和劳拉·布拉德利聊聊。"当道格拉斯的姨妈告诉我那个男孩得了白血病，"她说，"我感觉到了自己眼中的泪水。这使我想起了我最初知道我得白血病的时候。我清楚那个男孩必须经受什么。我想让他知道他真的可以好起来。所以我写了那张贺卡并装进了信封。我没告诉任何人。我在这里工作的时间不长，我怕

❺ **highpitched** /ˈhaɪˈpɪtʃd/ *adj.* (指声音)声调高的

❻ **beat the disease** 战胜疾病

"When Douglas's aunt told me that the boy had leukemia," she said, "I felt tears coming to my eyes. It reminded me of when I first learned that I had it. I realized what the boy must have been going through. I wanted him to know that he really can get better. So I wrote the card and slipped[7] it into the envelope. I didn't tell anyone. I haven't been working here very long, and I was afraid I might get in trouble."

It's funny. Douglas Maurer was in a hospital filled with millions of dollars of the most sophisticated medical equipment. He was being treated by expert doctors and nurses with medical training totaling hundreds of years. But it was a salesclerk in a flower shop, a woman making $170 a week, who — by taking the time to care, and by being willing to go with what her heart told her to do — gave Douglas hope and the will to carry on.

The human spirit can be an amazing thing, and sometimes you encounter it at its very best when you aren't even looking.

自己惹麻烦。”

这很有趣：道格拉斯·莫勒住在一个有成千上亿美元的最精密仪器的医院，这里有加起来一共受过几百年专业训练的专家医生和护士们为他治疗。但却是一个花店的售货员，每周挣170美元，通过关心以及发自内心的祝愿，给了道格拉斯希望和继续生活下去的毅力。

人们的精神是十分令人惊异的事物，有时甚至当你自己都没注意时，你发现它处于最佳状态。

❼ **slip**
/slɪp/
vt. 沿某方向顺畅而容易地移动

Relish[1] the moment

拥抱今天

The true joy of life is the trip. The station is only a dream. It constantly outdistances us.

生活的真正乐趣在于旅行的过程，而终点站不过是个梦，它始终在我们的前方。

Tucked away[2] in our subconscious[3] is an idyllic[4] vision. We see ourselves on a long trip that spans the continent. We are traveling by train. Out the windows, we drink in the passing scene of cars on nearby highways, of children waving at a crossing, of cattle grazing on a distant hillside, of smoke pouring from a power plant, of row upon row of corn and wheat, of flatlands and valleys, of mountains and rolling hillsides, of city skylines and village halls.

But uppermost in our minds is the final destination[5]. On a certain day at a certain hour, we will pull into the station. Bands will be playing and flags waving. Once we get there, so many wonderful dreams will come true and the pieces of our lives will fit together like a completed jigsaw[6] puzzle. How restlessly we pace the aisles[7], damning the minutes for loitering[8] — waiting, waiting, waiting for the station.

"When we reach the station that will be it!" We cry. "When I'm 18." "When I buy a new 450SL Mercedes Benz!" "When I put the last kid through college." "When I have paid off the mortgage[9]!" "When I get a promotion." "When I reach the age of retirement, I shall live happily ever after!"

Sooner or later, we must realize there is no station, no one place to arrive at once and for all. The true joy of life is the trip. The station is only a dream. It constantly outdistances us.

"Relish the moment" is a good motto[10], especially when

我们的潜意识里藏着一派田园诗般的风光。我们仿佛身处一次横贯大陆的漫漫旅程之中。乘着火车，我们领略着窗外流动的景色：附近高速公路上奔驰的汽车、十字路口处招手的孩童、远山上吃草的牛群、源源不断地从电厂排放出的浓烟、一片片的玉米和小麦、平原与山谷、群山与绵延的丘陵、天空映衬下城市的轮廓，以及乡间的庄园宅第。

然而我们心里想得最多的却是最终的目的地。在某一天的某一时刻，我们将会抵达终点站。迎接我们的将是乐队和飘舞的彩旗。一旦到了那儿，多少美梦将成为现实，我们的生活也将变得完整，如同一块摆好了的拼图。可是我们现在在过道里不耐烦地踱来踱去，咒骂火车的拖拖拉拉。我们期待着，期待着，期待着火车进站的那一刻。

“当我们到站的时候，一切就都好了！”我们呼喊着。“当我 18 岁的时候！”“当我有了一辆新 450SL 奔驰的时候！”“当我供最小的孩子念完大学的时候！”“当我偿清贷款的时候！”“当我官升高任的时候！”“当我到了退休的时候，就可以从此过上幸福的生活啦！”

可是我们终究会认识到人生的旅途中并

❶ **relish** /ˈrelɪʃ/
v. 享受(某事物)，从(某事物)中获得乐趣

❷ **tuck sth/oneself away**
将某物存起来或藏起来，躲藏

❸ **subconscious** /ˌsʌbˈkɒnʃəs/
adj. 下意识的，潜意识的

❹ **idyllic** /ɪˈdɪlɪk/
adj. 田园诗般的，田园风光的，平和欢畅的

❺ **destination** /ˌdestɪˈneɪʃn/
n. 目的地

❻ **jigsaw** /ˈdʒɪɡsɔː/
n. 拼图玩具

❼ **aisle** /aɪl/
n. 侧廊，过道

❽ **loiter** /ˈlɔɪtə/
v. 闲站着，慢走

❾ **mortgage** /ˈmɔːɡɪdʒ/
n. 押款，抵押

❿ **motto** /ˈmɒtəʊ/
n. 箴言，格言，座右铭

coupled with Psalm 118:24: "This is the day which the Lord hath made; we will rejoice and be glad in it. "It isn't the burdens of to day that drive men mad. It is the regrets over yesterday and the fear of tomorrow. Regret and fear are twin thieves who rob us of today.

So stop pacing the aisles and counting the miles. Instead, climb more mountains, eat more ice cream, go barefoot more often, swim more rivers, watch more sunsets, laugh more, cry less. Life must be lived as we go along. The station will come soon enough.

没有站，也没有能够“一到永逸”的地方！生活的真正乐趣在于旅行的过程，而终点站不过是个梦，它始终在我们的前方。

“享受现在”是句很好的箴言，尤其是当它与《圣经·诗篇》中第118页24行的一段话相映衬的时候，更是如此：“今日乃主所创造；生活在今日我们将欢欣、高兴。”真正令人发疯的不是今日的负担，而是对昨日的悔恨及对明日的恐惧。悔恨与恐惧是一对孪生窃贼，将今天从你我身边偷走。

那么就不要在过道里徘徊了，别老惦记着你离终点站还有多远。何不换一种活法，攀登更多的高山，多吃点儿冰淇淋，经常光着脚板儿溜达溜达，在更多的河流里畅游，多看看夕阳西下，多点欢笑，少点泪水。生活要前进。终点站就会很快到达。

Success: fact or fantasy[1]?

成功：现实还是幻想？

Pat yourself on the back. Toot your own horn. Don't adhere to anyone's opinion of success but your own.

拍拍自己的背，吹响你自己的号角，不要在意别人对成功的看法，坚持你自己对成功的理解。

Success. It's as alluring[2] as sin[3], as elusive[4] as the Muse. Is it real? Is it a dream or a fantasy? Who or what defines success? Webster's dictionary defines succeed as "to accomplish what is attempted" and success as "the attainment of wealth, etc."

As beauty is in the eyes of the beholder, so is success.

As beginning writers, we define success as finishing that first scene, chapter, story or manuscript. As we grow as writers, our definition of success grows. We begin to think of success in terms of writing something that makes sense, that makes someone smile, laugh or cry; something that touches the reader. When we become published we associate success with sales, reviews, contracts, $$$'s.

Success is measured in many ways, in small accomplishments and in large. There is no such thing as a small or moderate amount of success. Success is in and of itself; SUCCESS. It just is.

My book *Tempered Hearts* was electronically published in December 2000. Is that success? I've had one short story and one inspirational article in *The Romantic Bower Ezine*. Is that success? After writing for nineteen years and submitting for 8, I've actually begun to see a small income. A very slight return for the amount of time and money invested in this fickle[5] business called writing. Is that success?

Many people have said to me: "You should be proud, actu-

成功，它如同罪恶一样吸引人，像缪斯一样难以理解。它是真的吗？它是一场梦或一种幻想吗？由谁或什么定义成功？韦氏字典把成功定义为“实现尝试做的事情”和“获得财富，等等。”

成功因人而异，如同每个人眼中的漂亮都不一样。

作为刚刚起步的作家，我们把成功定义为完成一幕，一章，一个故事或一份手稿。随着作家的成长，我们对成功的定义也有了变化。我们开始认为成功是写出有意义的，让人们微笑、大笑或哭泣，能够感动读者的东西。当我们的书出版了，我们把成功与销量、评论、契约、金钱联系起来。

成功可以用不同的方法来衡量，可以是小的成就，也可以是大的成就。没有小成功或中等成功之分。成功就是成功本身，它就是它自己。

我的书《平和的心情》在 2000 年 12 月出了电子版。那是成功吗？我已经有一篇短故事和一篇鼓舞人心的文章发表在 *The Romantic Bower Ezine* 上。那是成功吗？在写了 19 年，递交了 8 次之后，我终于看到了一点儿小小的收入。在这个变化无常的叫做写作的生意中投入的时间和金钱得到了小小

❶ **fantasy** /ˈfæntəsɪ/ *n.* 想象，幻想
❷ **alluring** /əˈlʊərɪŋ/ *adj.* 吸引人的，迷人的，诱惑人的
❸ **sin** /sɪn/ *n.* 罪恶，严重过失
❹ **elusive** /ɪˈluːsɪv/ *adj.* 难以捉摸的，难以理解的
❺ **fickle** /ˈfɪkl/ *adj.* 易变的，无常的

ally writing a book is quite an accomplishment getting it published is quite another." AND "Ms. Thibodeaux has an outstanding career ahead of her." My book is getting reviews such as: "Steamier[6] and grittier[7] without decreasing the message" "A job well done" "An outstanding story of true love and the obstacles you have to overcome to realize loves permanence." Do these comments make me successful? Though I cringe[8] at the thought of being 'proud' I am very pleased and grateful for the success God has granted me thus far.

How do you define success? Is it more successful to write the book of your heart or write for the market? I believe success is in the heart. It is as personal as your relationship with God and with others.

Have you finished that rough draft, first chapter, and difficult scene? You are successful. Have you submitted to an agent or editor, signed that contract, made a few $$$'s? You are successful. Have you reached that goal, made new ones, are you steadily working toward them? You are successful.

Congratulate yourself. Pat yourself on the back. Toot[9] your own horn. Don't adhere to anyone's opinion of success but your own and take the time to enjoy each tiny accomplishment along the way. And remember: A man plans his way but God directs his steps.

的回报。那是成功吗？

许多人对我说："你应该感到骄傲，实际上写一本书已经很了不起了，出版之后就更了不起了，"而且"Thibodeaux 女士未来的事业会更出色。"有关我的书评包括："没有降低道德标准的情况下狂放而刚强"，"写得很好"，"一部关于真正的爱情及战胜困难认识爱情永恒的杰出作品"。是这些评论使我成功吗？尽管我对骄傲这一想法感到害怕，我很高兴也很感激上帝至今为止给予我的成功。

你如何定义成功？按照自己的心愿写书或为市场的需求写书，哪一个更成功一些？我相信成功存在于内心当中，它就像你跟上帝和你跟他人的关系一样个人化。

你完成草稿第一章和较难的一幕了吗？你是成功的。你向编辑交稿了吗？签合同了吗？挣到一点儿钱没有？你是成功的。你达到那个目标了吗？确定新的目标了吗？稳步向目标前进了吗？你是成功的。

祝贺你自己。拍拍自己的背，吹响你自己的号角，不要在意别人对成功的看法，坚持你自己对成功的理解，找时间庆祝一下成功路上的每个小成就。并且铭记："每个人都计划自己的路，但上帝指引他的脚步"。

⑥ **steamy** /ˈstiːmɪ/ *adj.* 狂放的

⑦ **gritty** /ˈɡrɪtɪ/ *adj.* 刚强的

⑧ **cringe** /krɪndʒ/ *v.* 退缩，畏缩

⑨ **toot** /tuːt/ *v.* （使某物）发嘟嘟声

Goals, attitude, belief in self make success

目标、态度、自信创造成功

A solid goal, a positive attitude and a strong belief would lead anybody who desires success along that path.

一个坚实的目标、积极的态度和坚定的信仰将引领任何渴望成功的人走上成功之路。

I have always wondered about the secrets of successful people. What do they have that lifts them above the ordinary? How do they achieve the superhuman feats that elevate them above others?

First of all, I must affirm my belief in the earlier part of the statement accredited[1] to Snowball in George Orwell's *Animal Farm* "All animals are equal..."

All human beings are indeed equal, but why does it seem as if some are more equal than others?

I have spent some time studying biographies and autobiographies of great men and women and have found some common denominators[2] among them all. I want to share some of them with you, hoping it will help you in your quest[3] for success.

The first common denominator is a solid goal.

Successful people know what they want and are willing to do everything necessary to get it. They set big, hairy[4], audacious[5] goals and believe in them so deeply that their lives naturally begin to gravitate[6] toward those goals.

Mohammed Ali decided he wanted to be the greatest athlete ever and told the world he was the greatest even before he won a championship fight.

Marion Jones announced that she was going to win five

我总是想知道成功人士的秘密，他们拥有什么使他们超越平凡呢？他们如何把自己提升到他人之上取得超人的功绩？

首先，我必须肯定，我相信乔治·奥威尔的《动物庄园》前面一部分中雪球所说的一句话“所有的动物都是平等的……”

所有人也的确是平等的，但为什么看起来好像一些人比其他人更平等呢？

我花了一些时间学习伟人的传记和自传，并且发现了他们的一些共同点。我想和你分享一下，希望这些对你追求成功有所帮助。

第一个共同点是：一个坚实的目标。

成功的人知道他们想要什么，并且愿意做所有必要的事情来获取成功。他们有远大的、困难的、无畏的目标，并对目标坚信不移，以至于他们的生命自然地开始向这些目标移动。

穆罕穆德·阿里甚至在他赢得拳击冠军之前就决定他想要成为最伟大的运动员，并向全世界宣称他是最伟大的。

马里恩·琼斯宣称他要在悉尼奥运会上赢得五块金牌。她只赢得了三块金牌两块铜牌。仅仅三金二铜。

第二，成功的人保持积极的态度。尽管有挫折他们仍相信自己的目标与抱负。

❶ **accredit** /əˈkredɪt/
v. 认为（某种说法等）出自某人，认为某人所（说等）

❷ **denominator** /dɪˈnɒmɪneɪtə/
n. 分母

❸ **quest** /kwest/
n. 寻求，寻找，追求

❹ **hairy** /ˈheərɪ/
adj. 困难的，令人不快的

❺ **audacious** /ɔːˈdeɪʃəs/
adj. 有冒险精神的；大胆的，无畏的

❻ **gravitate** /ˈgrævɪteɪt/
adj. 逐渐移向某事物，受…吸引

Olympic gold medals at the Sydney Olympics. She only won three gold and two bronze medals. Only three gold and two bronze medals.

Second, successful people maintain a positive attitude. They believe in their goals and aspirations[7] despite setbacks.

Perhaps the most famous example is former President Abraham Lincoln. He failed in business in 1831; he was defeated for a seat in the legislature[8] in 1832; he failed in business again in 1833; he suffered a nervous breakdown in 1836; he was defeated for speaker in 1838; he was defeated for elector in 1840; he lost his bid for Congress in 1843; he was defeated for vice president in 1856; he lost another run for the Senate in 1858; but he persevered.

He never gave up and was elected president in 1860. The rest, as they say, is history.

Third, successful people believe in themselves and a higher power. Success seems to favor those who have a healthy self-esteem and believe in a divinely endowed ability to achieve success and happiness.

The apostle Paul, a successful man who single handedly took the gospel around the then-known world, said in his letter to the Philippians, "I can do all things through Christ who strengthens me." In that statement he affirmed his belief in himself and in God, which gave him strength.

也许最有名的事例要数前总统亚伯拉罕·林肯了。他1831年生意失败，1832年竞选立法机关席位失败，1833年生意再次失败，1836年他由于紧张，身体累垮了；1838年竞选议长失败；1840年没能成为选民，1843年竞选国会失败，1856年竞选副总统失败，1858年竞选参议院席位再次失败，但是他坚持下来了。

他从没有放弃，并且在1861年被选为总统。剩下的，正像人们所说的，是历史了。

第三，成功的人相信他们自己并且有较强的能力。成功看来喜欢那些有正确自我意识并且相信神赋予他们能力追求成功和幸福的人。

使徒保罗，一个成功的人，他独自把福音带给了后世，在他写给腓力比书的信中说"有耶稣支持我，我可以做任何事情。"在这句话中他肯定了他对自己和耶稣的信任，这给了他力量。

本杰明·富兰克林，大概是人们描述过的最成功的人，说，"在所有合适的场合相信神是人类的义务……"

"成功"这个词被滥用并错误地译为巨大的财富和声望。我不同意。

使人同意好莱坞对成功的定义是真正意

❼ **aspiration**
/ˌæspəˈreɪʃn/
n. 渴望，抱负，志气

❽ **legislature**
/ˈledʒɪsleɪtʃə/
n. 立法机关，立法团体

Benjamin Franklin, who has been described as probably the most successful man who ever lived said, "It is the duty of mankind on all suitable occasions to acknowledge their dependence on the divine being..."

The word "success" has been abused[9] and wrongly translated to mean stupendous[10] wealth and fame. I beg to differ.

It is difficult to agree that Hollywood's definition of success is true success. The price (unhappiness) is too high.

I believe success is the progressive achievement of career, personal and family goals, all at the expense of none.

A solid goal, a positive attitude and a strong belief would lead anybody who desires success along that path.

义上的成功十分困难。代价（不幸）太高了。

我相信成功是事业、个人和家庭的目标上的逐步成就，不以牺牲任何一个为代价。

一个坚实的目标、积极的态度和坚定的信仰将引领任何渴望成功的人走上成功之路。

⑨ **abuse**
/əˈbjuːz/
v. 滥用，妄用

⑩ **stupendous**
/stjuːˈpendəs/
adj. 极大的，极好的

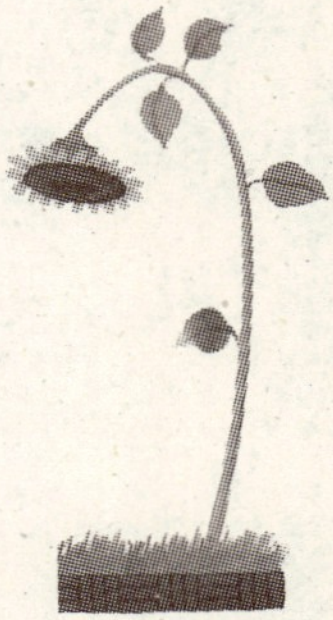

It's never too late

永远不晚

I want to thank you for calling me... for your sake.

我想谢谢你给我打电话——也是为了你自己的解脱。

Several years ago, while attending a communications course, I experienced[1] a most unusual process. The instructor asked us to list anything in our past that we felt ashamed of, guilty about, regretted, or incomplete about. The next week he invited participants to read their lists aloud. This seemed like a very private process, but there's always some brave soul in the crowd who will volunteer. As people read their lists, mine grew longer. After three weeks, I had 101 items on my list. The instructor then suggested that we find ways to make amends[2], apologize to people, or take some action to right any wrongdoing. I was seriously wondering how this could ever improve my communications, having visions of alienating[3] just about everyone from my life.

The next week, the man next to me raised his hand and volunteered this story:

"While making my list, I remembered an incident[4] from high school. I grew up in a small town in Iowa. There was a sheriff[5] in town that none of us kids liked. One night, my two buddies and I decided to play a trick on Sheriff Brown. After drinking a few beers, we found a can of red paint, climbed the tall water tank in the middle of town, and wrote, on the tank, in bright red letters: Sheriff Brown is an s.o.b.[6] The next day, the town arose to see our glorious[7] sign. Within two hours, Sheriff Brown had my two pals and me in his office. My friends confessed[8] and I lied, denying the truth. No one ever found out.

"Nearly 20 years later, Sheriff Brown's name appears on my

几年前，我参加了一个交际课程班，我体验了一段非常不同寻常的经历。教员要求我们列出过去所有让我们羞愧，内疚，遗憾或未完成的事情。第二周他邀请学员们大声朗读他们的清单。这看起来像一个不宜公开的事情，但众多人中总有一些勇敢的人自愿参加。当人们读他们的清单时，我的那份变得更长了。三周过后，我的清单上有101条。然后教员建议我们找一些途径来弥补，向人们道歉或采取行动改正错误的行为。我认真地想这怎么能够提高我们的交际能力，这样做只能众叛亲离。

又过了一周，坐在我旁边的那个人举手，自告奋勇地讲出了下面这个故事。

“当我写我的清单时，我想起了高中时的一件小事。我在依阿华州的一个小城中长大，这里有一个我们孩子们都不喜欢的治安官。一天晚上，我和我的两个朋友决定捉弄一下治安官布朗。喝了一点儿啤酒后，我们找了一桶漆，爬到城中心的大水罐上，用明亮的红漆写道：治安官布朗是一个s.o.b.。第二天，全城的人起来后都来看我们醒目的大标语。两小时内，治安官布朗派人把我和我的两个朋友带到了办公室。我的两个朋友承认了错误，而我撒了谎，没承认事实，也没

❶ **experience**
/ɪkˈspɪərɪəns/
v. 经历，经验

❷ **make amends**
（对所施加的污辱或损害）赔偿某人

❸ **alienate**
/ˈeɪlɪəneɪt/
v. 使某人疏远或冷淡，离间某人

❹ **incident**
/ˈɪnsɪdənt/
n. 事情，发生的事（常指小事）

❺ **sheriff**
/ˈʃerɪf/
n. 行政长官

❻ **s.o.b.**
= *son of bitch*

❼ **glorious**
/ˈglɔːrɪəs/
adj. 光荣的；光辉灿烂的

❽ **confess**
/ˈkənˈfes/
v. 承认错误，供认

list. I didn't even know if he was still alive. Last weekend, I dialed information in my hometown back in Iowa. Sure enough, there was a Roger Brown still listed. I dialed his number. After a few rings, I heard: 'Hello? ' I said:

'Sheriff Brown? ' Pause. 'Yup.' 'Well, this is Jimmy Calkins. And I want you to know that I did it.' Pause. 'I knew it! ' he yelled back. We had a good laugh and a lively discussion. His closing words were: 'Jimmy, I always felt badly for you because your buddies got it off their chest, and I knew you were carrying it around all these years. I want to thank you for calling me...for your sake.'"

Jimmy inspired me to clear up all 101 items on my list. It took me almost two years, but it became the springboard[9] and true inspiration for my career as a conflict mediator. No matter how difficult the conflict, crisis or situation, I always remember that it's never too late to clear up the past and begin resolution.

有人发现这件事。”

大约20年过去了，治安官布朗的名字出现在我的清单上。我甚至不知道他是否还活着。上周末，我打回电话到家乡依阿华州查资料。当然，这仍有一个罗杰·布朗。我拨了他的号码，响了几声之后，我听见：‘喂?’我说：‘治安官布朗吗?’停了一下。‘是。’‘嗯，我是吉米·考克斯。我想让你知道我过去做的那件事。’又停了一下。‘我早知道了!’他大声说道。我们开心地笑了，并愉快地聊了一会儿。他最后说：‘吉米，我总是为你感到难过，因为你的朋友们把事情从内心说了出来，而我知道你这些年一直在心里承受着这件事。我想谢谢你给我打电话——也是为了你自己的解脱。’”

吉米鼓励我处理好我清单上的101件事。这几乎花了我两年时间，但这件事变成了我从事矛盾调解员这个职业的发展起点和真正的鼓舞。不管矛盾、危机或情形多么困难，我总是记住清除过去的影响，并且开始解决问题，能这样做永远都不晚。

⑨ **springboard**
/ˈsprɪŋbɔːd/
n. 跳板；(比喻)发展事业的起点

Developing self-confidence

培养自信

Indeed, it is that very quality in humanity which refuses to stay defeated. A kind of stubborn cheerfulness.

实际上，它是人类不甘于失败的品质，一种绝不退让的快活。

Confidence is a feeling — an inner fire and an outer radiance[1], a basic satisfaction with what one is plus a reaching out to become more. Confidence is not something a few people are born with and others are not, for it is an acquired characteristic.

Confidence is the personal possession of no one; the person who has it learns it — and goes on learning. The most gifted individual on earth has to construct confidence in his gifts from the basis of faith and experience, like anybody else. The tools will differ from one person to the next, but the essential task is the same. Confidence and pose are available[2] to us all according to our abilities and needs — not somebody else's — provided we utilize our gifts and expand them.

One of the most rewarding[3] aspects of confidence is that it sits gracefully on every age and level of life — on children, men, women, the famous, the obscure[4], rich, poor, artist, executive, teen-ager, the very old. And you can take it with you into old age. There is nothing more inspiring than an old person who maintains his good will, humor, and faith in himself, in others, in the future. Conversely, the root cause of old people's despair is a feeling of not being wanted, of nothing to contribute, no more to conquer and become.

Most people have more to work with than they realize. One noted physicist calls this unused excellencies and finding and releasing this potential in ourselves is one of the major challenges of modern life. The great danger is not that we shall overreach our

自信是一种感觉——一种来自内心的火焰和外在的灿烂，使人们可以获得更多基本的满足感。自信不是某些人天生就有而另一些人没有，它是后天培养起来的性格。

自信不是任何人的私有财产；人们通过学习获得自信并且坚持继续学习。这个世界上最聪明的人也要像其他人一样，在信念和经历的基础上来培养自信。一个人和另一个人用的工具可能不同，但是核心的任务是一样的。倘若运用我们的才智并使之不断增长，依靠我们自己的而不是别人的能力和需求，我们就可以做到自信和沉着冷静。

自信最令人满意的方面之一是它不分年龄和生活水准不懈地跟随我们每个人——小孩，男人，女人，名人，平凡人，富人，穷人，艺术家，行政人员，青少年，老人。你还可以把自信带入老年。再没有比一个老人能够保持对自己，对别人和未来怀有美好意愿、心情、信念更能鼓舞人心的了。相反，老人绝望的根本原因是不被需要，无所贡献，无所征服和无所成就的感觉。

大多数人都比他们意识到的更大有可为。一位著名的物理学家把它称之为未被利用的优点，找到并且释放我们身上的这些潜能是当代生活中重要的挑战之一。最多的危险不

❶ **radiance**
/ˈreɪdɪəns/
n. 发光，灿烂，容光焕发

❷ **available**
/əˈveɪləbl/
adj. 可用的或可得到的，有用的

❸ **rewarding**
/rɪˈwɔːdɪŋ/
adj. （指活动等）值得做的，令人满意的

❹ **obscure**
/əbˈskjʊə/
adj. 不著名的

capacities but that we shall undervalue and under-employ them, thus blighting[5] our great possibilities.

The goal of life is not a problemless existence, which would be unbearably dull, but a way to handle problems creatively. That word "problem" may sound a little prickly, but it only means a question put forth for solution, and actually life consists of a series of problems-and-solutions, each different from the last.

Confidence is delight — delight[6] in living, in being who you are, in what you do, in growing, in the endless and sometimes exasperating[7] adventure of what it means to be human. The teacher who delights in teaching has no time for bogging down[8] in a swamp of doubt that he or she is doing it "right," and they are well aware that they can become a better teacher tomorrow, but only by doing their best today and enjoying today. So, too, the mother who delights in being a mother does not worry overmuch about whether she fits the rules. She is not the mother, after all, of something material but of a living child.

Rules can often be a guide to successful living, but they are not a substitute for living. Rules never quite keep up with reality, because rules come from experience, not the other way around. Life happens, and it is infinitely inventive. It will always outrun and outmaneuver[9] any attempt to bottle it up[10] in a cut-and-dried system, for life is perpetual becoming. When life turns your wisest plans or best rules upside down, throw out the plans and bend with the circumstance. You will find powers you did not suspect,

是我们高估我们的能力，而是我们会低估并且不能充分利用这些能力，这会破坏我们的潜能。

生活的目标不是无忧无虑，那样会无聊得无法忍受，而应该是创造性地解决问题。“问题”这个词可能听起来有点让人生气，但是它只意味着一个被提出的等待解决的问题，事实上生活就是由一系列的问题——解决问题构成的，每一个问题都与上一个不同。

自信是喜悦，生活的喜悦，是自我的快乐，做事的快乐，成长的快乐，体验人类种种坎坷历程的快乐。以教学为快乐的老师，没有时间怀疑他（她）做得是否对，通过今天的努力工作并感到满意，他们很清楚明天会做得更好。母亲也如此，她们也不会过多地担心她是否适合这个角色。她照顾的毕竟不是无生命的物质，而是一个活生生的孩子。

规则是通往成功生活的向导，但不是生活的替代品。规则不是十分符合现实，因为规则来自于经验，而不是经验来自规则。生活的真谛远胜于发明创造。生活总会超越那些束缚它的一板一眼的制度，因为生活总在变化。当生活把你最聪明的计划或最好的准则推翻时，扔掉那些计划，适应环境，你会找到你意想不到的力量，以及你做梦也没想

❺ **blight** /blaɪt/
v. 损坏，损害

❻ **delight**
/dɪˈlaɪt/
n. 高兴，快乐，喜悦

❼ **exasperating**
/ɪɡˈzæspəreɪtɪŋ/
adj. 使人极恼怒的，使人发火的

❽ **bog down**
（使某物）陷入困境不能前进

❾ **outmaneuver**
/ˌaʊtməˈnuːvə/
v. 比（对手等）技高一着，智高一筹

❿ **bottle sth. up**
掩盖（情绪），抑制（感情）

and possibilities undreamed of.

Confidence is not always winning, not always victory. Indeed, it is that very quality in humanity which refuses to stay defeated. A kind of stubborn[11] cheerfulness. Remember there are two things you can do with mistakes: you can run away and you can grow.

到的可能性。

自信并不是总能胜利，总能打赢。实际上，它是人类不甘于失败的品质，一种绝不退让的快活。记住对于错误你可以采取两种态度：你可以逃避，也可以从中成长。

⑪ **stubborn**
/ˈstʌbən/
adj. 不退让的，倔强的

Follow your dream

追随你的梦想

Don't let anyone steal your dreams. Follow your heart, no matter what.

不要让任何人偷走你的梦想。抓住你心中所向往的，无论那是什么。

I have a friend named Monty Roberts who owns a horse ranch[1] in San Ysidro. He has let me use his house to put on fund-raising events to raise money for youth at risk programs.

The last time I was there he introduced me by saying, "I want to tell you why I let Jack use my house. It all goes back to a story about a young man who was the son of an itinerant[2] horse trainer who would go from stable[3] to stable, race track to race track, farm to farm and ranch to ranch, training horses. As a result, the boy's high school career was continually interrupted. When he was a senior, he was asked to write a paper about what he wanted to be and do when he grew up.

"That night he wrote a seven-page paper describing his goal of someday owning a horse ranch. He wrote about his dream in great detail and he even drew a diagram of a 200-acre[4] ranch, showing the location of all the buildings, the stables and the track. Then he drew a detailed floor plan for a 4,000-square-foot house that would sit on a 200-acre dream ranch.

"He put a great deal of his heart into the project and the next day he handed it in to his teacher. Two days later he received his paper back. On the front page was a large red F with a note that read, 'See me after class.'"

"The boy with the dream went to see the teacher after class and asked, 'Why did I receive an F?'

我有一个朋友叫蒙蒂·罗伯特，他在圣伊塞德罗有一个牧马场。他让我用他的房子搞集资活动为那些进行冒险的年轻人筹款。

最后一次，在蒙蒂的牧场他这样介绍我说，“我想告诉你们我为什么让杰克用我的房子。这要回到一个年轻人的故事上，这个年轻人是一个流动驯马员的儿子，这个驯马员到处驯马，从一个马厩到另一个马厩，从一个赛场到另一个赛场，从一个农场到另一个农场，从一个牧场到另一个牧场。结果使孩子的高中生活常常被打断。当这个孩子成为一个高中生时，他被要求写一篇关于他长大以后想做什么的文章。”

“那个晚上，他写了7页纸描述他将来某一天拥有一个牧场的目标。他详细地写下了他的梦想，甚至画了一幅200英亩的牧场图，展示所有的房子，马厩和跑道的位置。然后他详尽计划了坐落在200英亩梦想的牧场上的4 000平方英尺的房子。”

“他尽全力来完成这个工程，并且第二天交给了老师。两天后他拿回的自己的文章。在第一页上有一个大大的红色的F，并且还写着‘下课后来找我。’”

“课后，男孩带着他的梦想去见老师，并问，‘为什么给我F?’”

❶ **ranch** /rɑːntʃ/ *n.* 牧场，饲养场
❷ **itinerant** /aɪˈtɪnərənt/ *adj.* 巡回的，流动的
❸ **stable** /ˈsteɪbl/ *n.* 马厩
❹ **acre** /ˈeɪkə/ *n.* 英亩

"The teacher said, 'This is an unrealistic dream for a young boy like you. You have no money. You come from an itinerant family. You have no resources. Owning a horse ranch requires a lot of money. You have to buy the land. You have to pay for the original breeding stock and later you'll have to pay large stud[5] fees. There's no way you could ever do it.' Then the teacher added, 'If you will rewrite this paper with a more realistic goal, I will reconsider your grade.'

"The boy went home and thought about it long and hard. He asked his father what he should do. His father said, 'Look, son, you have to make up your own mind on this. However, I think it is a very important decision for you.'"

"Finally, after sitting with it for a week, the boy turned in the same paper, making no changes at all. He stated, 'You can keep the F and I'll keep my dream.'"

Monty then turned to the assembled group and said, "I tell you this story because you are sitting in my 4,000-square-foot house in the middle of my 200-acre horse ranch. I still have that school paper framed over the fireplace[6]. "He added," The best part of the story is that two summers ago that same schoolteacher brought 30 kids to camp out on my ranch for a week." When the teacher was leaving, he said, 'Look, Monty, I can tell you this now. When I was your teacher, I was something of a dream stealer. During those years I stole a lot of kids' dreams. Fortunately you had enough gumption[7] not to give up on yours.'"

“老师说，‘对于一个像你这样的小孩来说这是一个不切实际的梦想。你没有钱，你来自一个流动的家庭，你没有资源。拥有一个牧场需要有很多钱。你要买地，要支付开始养牲畜的钱，之后你将要支付一笔种马钱。你根本没办法做到这些。’然后老师又说，‘如果你重新写这篇文章，写一个现实点儿的目标，我会再考虑你的分数。’”

“男孩回到家，冥思苦想了很长时间。他问父亲他应该怎么做。他父亲说，‘看，儿子，你必须自己决定这件事。尽管如此，我认为这对于你来说是一个非常重要的决定。’”

“最后，男孩又拿着这篇文章想了一周之后，男孩把同样的文章交了上去，没有任何改动。他说：‘你可以留着F，但我继续要我的梦想。’”

然后，蒙蒂转向聚集在一起的人说：“我告诉你们这个故事，因为你们现在正坐在我200英亩的牧场中心的4 000平方英尺的房子中。我仍留着那篇上学时的文章，镶好了挂在壁炉的上方。”他接着说，“故事最精彩的部分是，两年前那个老师带了30名学生在我的牧场上露营了一周。当老师要走时，他说：‘看，蒙蒂，现在我可以告诉你，当

❺ **stud** /stʌd/
n. 种马

❻ **fireplace** /ˈfaɪəpleɪs/
n. 壁炉

❼ **gumption** /ˈɡʌmpʃn/
n 常识与进取精神，魄力

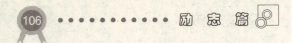

Don't let anyone steal your dreams. Follow your heart, no matter what.

我是你的老师时，我有点儿像梦想的偷窃者。在这些年间，我偷了很多孩子的梦想。幸运的是你有足够的魄力不放弃你的梦想。'”

不要让任何人偷走你的梦想。抓住你心中所向往的，无论那是什么。

Courage is a gift

勇气是才能

Live life in a constant state of awareness, with peaceful thoughts, a dash of forcefulness, and a good measure of faith and spirituality.

要生活在不断思考中，带着平静的思想，坚强的性格以及适当的信念和信仰。

Courage is daring to be Brave. Enterprising. Bold. In your business or personal life, how often do you question your thoughts, your actions, or your motives? When you don't exercise the ability to always test yourself, you may lose not only your confidence, but more importantly, you lose the ability to focus[1], to know yourself, your friends, and your customers.

When faced with decisions and challenges, asking yourself questions every day, every hour, every moment gives you the courage to discover what is important to you and what a particular situation means to you, and what result or solution you will like to accomplish.

Not many people experience life the way they want it to be. If things don't work out the way you want, don't find someone else to blame. Know what goals you want, then question your actions in reaching them. Compare your answers to what others may wish for you. After all, having a successful business or a life of contentment requires you to know yourself and the goals that are best for you.

Courage is getting in the habit of looking inward and going with your highest feeling of what is true and what feels right for you. Apply this inner evaluation in your business and in your personal life. This is important if you wish to grow and stay successful. It works!

Have the courage to be curious (not nosy[2]!). A quest[3] for

勇气是敢于面对风险，敢于进取，敢于无畏地前进。在你的工作或个人生活中，你时常对你的思想、行动或动机提出疑问吗？当你不经常锻炼检验自己的能力时，你不仅会失去信心，更重要的是，你会失去认识自己，认识你的朋友和顾客的能力。

当你面对决策与挑战时，时时刻刻都问你自己一些问题，这样做会给你勇气，发掘什么对于你来说是重要的；某个特殊的情况对于你意味着什么，以及你想达到什么样的结果，或找到什么样的解决办法。

不是很多人都能按照他们的理想来生活。如果事情和你想象的不一样，不要责备别人，想想你希望达到的目标，然后检查一下你追求目标的行动是否得当。比较你的回答和他人对你的期望。毕竟，工作的成功或生活的美满要求你要了解你自己和最适合于你的目标。

勇气是养成自省和找到对自己真正适合的感觉的习惯。如果你想成长并且保持成功，把这种自我评价应用到你的工作和个人生活中十分重要。这种方法的确有效。

要有勇气保持好奇心（但不要过分！）。寻求生活知识以及了解与你交往的人是有好处的。寻求你想做的每件事的答案。这使你

❶ **focus** /ˈfəʊkəs/ *v.* 能够看清楚

❷ **nosy** /ˈnəʊzɪ/ *adj.* 过分好奇的，爱管闲事的

❸ **quest** /kwest/ *n.* 寻求，追求

knowledge about life and the people you interact[4] with is good. Look for answers to whatever you plan to do. This keeps you thoughtful. Keep a journal if it helps. Over time, you can look back and discover the results of your actions (or reactions) to certain problems. Then when faced with future or similar problems, you'll have a ready solution.

Realize your weaknesses and work toward improving them. Continue to renew yourself and remember that life has a way of constantly testing your ability and courage to deal with it. When you can learn to appreciate the challenges in both your business and personal life, you find inner strength. Then you are able to bring about an inner peace and spirituality[5] that gives you a good tool for building self-confidence and self esteem.

There is something inside each of us that fuels our motivation, our passion, and our reason to succeed. Keep encouraging yourself to take the necessary risks to refuel your confidence. Question your motives. Then search for the answer. Question any doubts you or others may have about your courage to succeed. You are what is important.

Don't let negative thoughts get in the way of your progress and your goals. Control your thoughts. Think about what is important to you. When your thoughts are positive, they have a way of replenishing[6] your courage. No matter how often unpleasant or difficult challenges get you down, don't give in to negative thinking. Just pick yourself up and move on. Focus on what gives you

更能顾及他人的需要。如果有帮助的话，可以记日记。过一段时间，你可以回过头去看看，发现针对某个问题你的行动（或反应）所产生的结果。这样当面对未来或同样的问题时，你则有备无患。

认识你的弱点并且尽力改善它们。不断赋予你自己新的生命与活力，并且记住生活总是不断检验你处理它的能力和勇气。当你学会欣赏工作和个人生活中的挑战时，你就会有来自内心的力量，之后你就可以得到内心的平静与精神的力量，这样便能更好地培养自信与自尊。

我们每个人的内心都有一些事物可以激发我们的动机、热情和理智来获取成功。不断鼓励你自己冒必要的风险来增强信心。检查一下你的动机，然后寻找答案，你有勇气成功，不要相信你自己或他人对此的怀疑。你是重要的。

不要让消极的思想妨碍你进步或达到目标。控制你的思想。想想对你重要的事情。当你的思想积极时，它们可以使你再次鼓起勇气。不管不愉快的或困难的挑战多么频繁地使你情绪低落，不要屈服于消极的思想。只需要站起来继续前进，把精力集中在给你力量和独特性的事物上。

❹ **interact**
/ˌɪntərˈækt/
v. 一起交往，互相合作

❺ **spirituality**
/ˌspɪrɪtʃʊˈælətɪ/
n. 精神性，灵性，信仰

❻ **replenish**
/rɪˈplenɪʃ/
v. 再将某物充满

your strength and uniqueness.

Remember：motivation, passion, and your reason to succeed in life, as well as in business, are essential requirements to reaching your goals. Live life in a constant state of awareness, with peaceful thoughts, a dash[7] of forcefulness, and a good measure of faith and spirituality. You will then be exercising your gift of courage.

记住：在生活中和工作中取得成功的动机、热情和理智，是达到你的目标必不可少的条件。要生活在不断思考中，带着平静的思想，坚强的性格以及适当的信念和信仰。这样你就可以磨练你的勇气。

⑦ **dash**
/dæʃ/
n. 活力，精力，干劲

Ask for what you want

争取梦想实现

Many people fail before they even begin because they fail to ask for what they want.

许多人还没有开始就已经失败了，因为他们不敢争取他们想要的东西。

The greatest saleswoman in the world today doesn't mind if you call her a girl. That's because Markita Andrews has generated[1] more than eighty thousand dollars selling Girl Scout cookies since she was seven years old.

Going door-to-door after school, the painfully shy Markita transformed herself into a cookie-selling dynamo[2] when she discovered at age 13, the secret of selling.

It starts with desire. Burning, white-hot desire.

For Markita and her mother, who worked as a waitress[3] in New York after her husband left them when Markita was eight years old, their dream was to travel the globe. "I'll work hard to make enough money to send you to college," her mother said one day. "You'll go to college and when you graduate[4], you'll make enough money to take you and me around the world. Okay?"

So at age 13, when Markita read in her Girl Scout magazine that the Scout who sold the most cookies would win an all-expenses-paid trip for two around the world, she decided to sell all the Girl Scout cookies she could — more Girl Scout cookies than anyone in the world, ever.

But desire alone is not enough. To make her dream come true, Markita knew she needed a plan.

"Always wear your right outfit[5], your professional garb[6]," her

当今世界上最伟大的女推销员可不会介意你喊她小姑娘，因为自从玛吉塔·安德鲁斯7岁时起，她已经靠推销女童军饼干赚了8万多美元。

13岁那年，她发现了推销的秘诀。通过放学后挨家挨户的推销，一向害羞得要命的玛吉塔已经变成了卖饼干的楷模。

这起源于一个愿望，一个强烈而热切的愿望。

在玛吉塔8岁的时候，父亲离开了她们，此后母亲在纽约作女服务员，他们母女俩的梦想就是要环游世界。"我要努力工作，赚足够的钱供你上大学，"一天，母亲说，"你会上大学的，等你大学毕业后，就赚足够的钱让我们环游世界，好吗？"

在玛吉塔13岁那年，《女童军》杂志发布消息说销售饼干最多的女童军队员将可获得两人免费全球旅游作为奖励，于是玛吉塔决定尽全部力量推销女童军饼干，要比世界上任何人卖得都多。

但仅有愿望是不够的，玛吉塔知道她要梦想成真就必须制定一个计划。

"当你去做生意时要穿得像做生意的样子，要随时随地穿得体的套装和职业服装，穿上你的女童军制服。在4:30或6:30去推

❶ **generate** /ˈdʒenəreɪt/ *v.* 混合的，合成的

❷ **dynamo** /ˈdaɪnəməʊ/ *n.* 精力充沛的人，干劲十足的人

❸ **waitress** /ˈweɪtrɪs/ *n.* 女服务员

❹ **graduate** /ˈɡrædʒʊət/ *v.* 毕业

❺ **outfit** /ˈaʊtfɪt/ *n.* 一套衣服（尤指适用于某种场合的）

❻ **garb** /ɡɑːb/ *n.* 服装

aunt advised. "When you are doing business, dress like you are doing business. Wear your Girl Scout uniform. When you go up to people in their tenement[7] buildings at 4:30 or 6:30 and especially on Friday night, ask for a big order. Always smile, whether they buy or not, always be nice. And don't ask them to buy your cookies; ask them to invest[8]."

Lots of other Scouts may have wanted that trip around the world. Lots of other Scouts may have had a plan. But only Markita went off in her uniform each day after school, ready to ask-and keep asking-folks to invest in her dream. "Hi, I have a dream. I'm earning a trip around the world for me and my mom by merchandising Girl Scout cookies," She'd say at the door. "Would you like to invest in one dozen or two dozen boxes of cookies?"

Markita sold 3,526 boxes of Girl Scout cookies that year and won her trip around the world. Since then, she has sold more than 42,000 boxes of Girl Scout cookies, spoken at sales conventions across the country, starred in a Disney movie about her adventure and has co-authored the best seller, *How to Sell More Cookies, Condos, Cadillacs, Computers…And Everything Else.*

Markita is no smarter and no more extroverted[9] than thousands of other people, young and old, with dreams of their own. The difference is Markita had discovered the secret of selling: Ask, Ask, Ask! Many people fail before they even begin because they fail to ask for what they want. The fear of rejection[10] leads many of us to reject ourselves and our dreams long before anyone else

销，尤其是星期五晚上去登门推销时，要争取大订单。不管他们买不买，要随时面带微笑，令人愉快。而且不要让他们‘买’你的饼干，要请求他们投资。”她的姨妈建议说。

可能有许多其他女童军队员也想去环球旅游，可能许多人都有计划。但只有玛吉塔每天放学后都穿着制服，随时随地锲而不舍地请求人们为她的梦想投资。“嗨，我有一个梦想，我想通过出售女童军饼干为我和妈妈赢得一次环球旅行，”她会站在门口说，“你愿意投资买进一或两打盒装的饼干吗?”

那一年玛吉塔共卖出 3 526 盒女童军饼干，赢得了环球旅行。从那时候到现在，她已经卖出了四万两千多盒女童军饼干，还在全国的众多销售会议上发言，主演了一部讲述自己的经历的迪斯尼电影，并与人合著了一本畅销书《如何售出更多的饼干、楼盘、汽车、计算机以及其他的一切》。

比起其他成千上万的拥有梦想的人，无论老人还是小孩，玛吉塔并不比他们聪明，也没有他们那么活泼开朗。不同之处在于玛吉塔发现了销售的秘诀：请求！请求！再请求！许多人还没有开始就已经失败了，因为他们不敢争取他们想要的东西。害怕被拒绝

⑦ **tenement** /ˈtenəmənt/ *n.* 公寓

⑧ **invest** /ɪnˈvest/ *v.* 投资

⑨ **extroverted** /ˈekstrəvɜːtɪd/ *adj.* 性格外向的

⑩ **rejection** /rɪˈdʒekʃn/ *n.* 拒绝

ever has the chance — no matter what we are selling.

And everyone is selling something. “You're selling yourself everyday — in school, to your boss, to new people you meet,” said Markita at 14. “My mother is a waitress: she sells the daily special. Mayors and presidents trying to get votes are selling... I see selling everywhere I look. Selling is part of the whole world.”

It takes courage to ask for what you want. Courage is not the absence[11] of fear. It's doing what it takes despite one's fear. And, as Markita has discovered, the more you ask, the easier (and more fun) it gets.

使我们许多人在被别人拒绝之前，就已经先否定了自己和自己的梦想，无论我们推销的是什么。

其实每个人都在推销一些东西。“每天你都在推销着自己，在学校推销、向你的老板推销、向你新结识的人推销，”14 岁的玛吉塔这样说，“我的母亲是个服务员，她推销每日特餐；为了获得选票，市长和总统也在进行推销……在我所有可以看到的地方我都可以看到推销。推销是整个世界的一部分。”

去争取达到你的梦想的确需要勇气。勇气不是没有恐惧感。正如玛吉塔所发现的那样，尽管你害怕，也要去争取，你请求的次数越多，你就越容易得到，也越有乐趣。

⓫ **absence** /ˈæbsəns/ *n.* 离开；不在某处

Self-assertion

说出你的想法

Self-worth comes from believing that you are a worthwhile individual who deserves the best that life has to offer.

自我肯定即相信你是一个应该得到生命中最美好事物的有价值的人。

Have you ever walked away from a situation and wished you handled it differently? At times, do you feel that others overlook your rights? Can you recall losing your temper and not getting your point across effectively? If you have answered "yes" to any of these questions, you may feel challenged in the area of assertiveness. Assertiveness is the ability to clearly represent your thoughts and feelings in a mutually respectful way. It does not infringe on[1] the rights of others or rely on guilt for results. Assertiveness starts with the premise[2] that each human being is given rights that do not depend on status or performance. You have the right to express your perspective. You have the right to assume personal responsibility and to decline responsibility for others. How you govern yourself in relation to these rights is important for "valued" communication.

Communication is valued when both parties, the sender and the receiver, are respected. There are three primary styles of communication: passive, assertive, and aggressive. The difference between passive, assertive, and aggressive communication rests with the exchange between parties and quality of the message. Passiveness diminishes your capacity to be heard and validated[3]. Aggressiveness exerts differential power to promote a certain end result that is not based on mutual respect. Only assertiveness respectfully engages both parties for valued communication.

In order to achieve assertive communication, one needs a level of self-confidence, self-worth, and self-awareness. Self-confidence is projected, not performed. It has to radiate[4] from within

你是否曾经逃避过某些事情而希望自己能以不同的方式处理呢？有时你是不是觉得别人忽略了你的权利？你是否曾经发脾气而你要表达的意思没能被人理解？如果你对以上任何一个问题作了肯定回答，你可能在自信方面遇到了挑战。自信是以互相尊重的方式清楚地表述你的看法和感受的能力。它不侵犯别人的权利也不因结果的错误而悔恨。自信的前提是每个人无论其地位或表现都被赋予权利。你有权表达你的看法。你有权对自己负责并拒绝为别人承担责任。你如何处理自己和这些权利的关系对有价值的交流很重要。

只有当说话的人和收听者双方都被尊重时，交流才有意义。有三种基本交流方式：消极被动的，坚定自信的和坚持己见的。这三种交流方式的不同点在于交流的双方和信息的质量。消极被动减弱了你被听到和被认可的能力。坚持己见运用不同的力量提倡不是建立在互相尊重基础上的结局。只有坚定自信才能使双方都能进行有效的交流。

为了达到坚定而自信地交流，每个人需要有一定程度的自信，自我肯定和自知之明。自信是反映出来的而不是表现出来的。他来自内心而且不依靠别的事物。自我肯定即相

❶ **infringe on**
侵犯，侵入，侵害

❷ **premise**
/ˈpremɪs/
n. 前提，假定

❸ **validate**
/ˈvælɪdeɪt/
v. 批准，认可

❹ **radiate**
/ˈreɪdɪeɪt/
v. 显露

and does not rely on[5] others. Self-worth comes from believing that you are a worthwhile individual who deserves the best that life has to offer. Self-awareness develops from personal monitoring. One learns of strengths and weaknesses by making internal assessments. Self-assertion is a natural process for individuals who are confident and aware. In essence[6], you must have confidence within before you can demonstrate it in the midst of others.

信你是一个应该得到生命中最美好事物的有价值的人。自知之明是通过自我监督培养起来的。通过内心的衡量一个人知道自己的长处和短处。有信心表达自己的看法对于有信心且了解自己的人是一个自然的过程。核心是，在你证明给别人看之前你必须有信心。

❺ **rely on**
依靠,依赖
❻ **in essence**
大体上,本质上

Attitude

态 度

Each morning I wake up and say to myself, you have two choices today.

每天早晨我起来对自己说，你今天有两个选择。

Michael is the kind of guy you love to hate. He is always in a good mood and always has something positive to say. When someone would ask him how he was doing, would reply, "If I were any better, I would be twins!"

He was a natural motivator. If an employee was having a bad day, Michael was there telling the employee how to look on the positive side of the situation.

Seeing this style[1] really made me curious[2], so one day I went up to Michael and asked him, "I don't get it! You can't be a positive person all of the time. How do you do it?" Michael replied, "Each morning I wake up and say to myself, you have two choices today. You can choose to be in a good mood or...you can choose to be in a bad mood. I choose to be in a good mood. Each time something bad happens, I can choose to be a Victim[3] or I can choose to learn from it. I choose to learn from it. Every time someone comes to me complaining, I can choose to accept their complaining or... I can point out the positive side of life. I choose the positive side of life."

"Yeah, right, it's not that easy," I protested[4].

"Yes, it is," Michael said. "Life is all about choices. When you cut away all the junk[5], every situation is a choice. You choose how you react to situations. You choose how people affect your mood. You choose to be in a good mood or bad mood. The bottom line: It's your choice how you live your life."

迈克尔是那种让你爱恨交织的人。他总是心情愉快并且总是说一些积极的话。当有人问他怎么样时，他会回答："如果我能更好的话，我就成双胞胎了！"

他是一个天生的鼓舞者。如果一个雇员某一天不顺利的话，迈克尔会过来告诉他如何看到情形积极的一面。

看到这种作风，真的使我很惊奇，所以，有一天我找到迈克尔并问他："我不明白！你不可能总是一个乐观的人。你是如何做到的？"迈克尔回答："每天早晨我起来对自己说，你今天有两个选择。你可以选择心情好或者……你可以选择心情不好。我选择心情好。每次发生一些不好的事情，我可以选择做一个牺牲者，或者我可以选择从中学习一些教训。我选择从中学习。每次有人走过来向我抱怨，我可以选择接受他们的抱怨或者……我可以指出生活积极的一面。我选择生活积极的一面。"

"是，对，这并不那么简单。"我反驳说。

"是的，就是这样。"迈克尔说，"生活总是在选择。排除那些盘根错节，每种情形都是一种选择。你选择如何对情况做出反应。你选择人们如何影响你的心情。你选择心情

❶ **style** /staɪl/ *n.* 行为方式，作风

❷ **curious** /ˈkjʊərɪəs/ *adj.* 奇怪的，惊奇的

❸ **victim** /ˈvɪktɪm/ *n.* 受害人，牺牲者

❹ **protest** /prəˈtest/ *v.* 抗议，异议，反对

❺ **junk** /dʒʌŋk/ *n.* 无用或无价值的东西

I reflected on what Michael said. Soon hereafter[6], I left the Tower Industry to start my own business. We lost touch, but I often thought about him when I made a choice about life instead of reacting to it.

Several years later, I heard that Michael was involved in a serious accident, falling some 60 feet from a communications tower. After 18 hours of surgery and weeks of intensive care, Michael was released from the hospital with rods[7] placed in his back.

I saw Michael about six months after the accident. When I asked him how he was, he replied. "If I were any better, I'd be a twin. Wanna see my scars?"

"The first thing that went through my mind was the well being of my soon to be born daughter," Michael replied. "Then, as I lay on the ground, I remembered that I had two choices: I could choose to live or... I could choose to die. I chose to live."

"Weren't you scared? Did you lose consciousness?" I asked.

Michael continued, "...the paramedics were great. They kept telling me I was going to be fine. But when they wheeled me into the ER and I saw the expressions on the faces of the doctors and nurses, I got really scared. In their eyes, I read, 'he's a dead man.' I knew I needed to take action."

"What did you do?" I asked.

好或者心情坏。底线是：你要如何生活是你的选择。”

我反思迈克尔说的话。不久以后，我离开了 Tower Industry 去开创我自己的生意。我们失去了联系，但是当我选择生活而不是让生活选择我时，我经常想到他。

几年过后，我听说迈克尔遭遇了一场严重的意外事故，从一个约 60 英尺的通信塔上摔了下来。18 小时的手术以及几周的特重看护后，迈克尔背上带着金属棒出院了。

意外发生大约 6 个月后，我见到了迈克尔。当我问他怎么样时，他说：“如果我能更好的话，我就成双胞胎了。想看看我的伤疤吗？”

“我大脑中闪现的第一件事是我即将出生的女儿的健康，”迈克尔说，“然后，当我躺在地上时，我想起我有两个选择：我可以选择生存或者……我可以选择死亡。我选择了生存。”

“你难道不害怕吗？你失去知觉了吗？”我问。

迈克尔继续说，“……护理员非常好。他们不断告诉我，我会好起来。但当他们把我推进急诊室，我看到医生和护士脸上的表情时，我真的害怕了。在他们眼中，我看到

❻ **hereafter** /ˌhɪərˈɑːftə/ *adv.* 从此以后，今后

❼ **rod** /rɒd/ *n.* （木质或金属的）杆，棒，棍

"Well, there was a big burly[8] nurse shouting questions at me," said Michael. "She asked if I was allergic[9] to anything."

"'Yes,' I replied. The doctors and nurses stopped working as they waited for my reply. I took a deep breath and yelled, 'Gravity[10].'

"Over their laughter, I told them, 'I am choosing to live. Operate on me as if I am alive, not dead.'"

Michael lived, thanks to the skill of his doctors, but also because of his amazing attitude. I learned from him that every day we have the choice to live fully.

'他是个死人。' 我知道我需要采取行动。"

"你干了什么?" 我问。

"是这样，有个高大健壮的护士大声问我," 迈克尔说。"她问我是否对什么过敏?"

"'是的,' 我答道。医生和护士停止了工作等待我的答案。我深吸一口气大声说道: '对地心引力过敏。'"

"在他们的笑声中，我告诉他们，'我选择生存。把我当成活人医治，而不是死人。'"

迈克尔活过来了，多亏那些医生的医术，但也缘于迈克尔那不可思议的态度。我从他身上学到这一点，每天我们都可以选择充实地生活。

❽ **burly** /ˈbɜːlɪ/
adj. 魁梧的，结实的，健壮的

❾ **allergic** /əˈlɜːdʒɪk/
adj. 过敏的，患过敏症的

❿ **gravity** /ˈgrævətɪ/
n. 地心引力，重力，万有引力

Stand up for yourself

为你自己而站立

Mom was right. You can' t reach for the stars if you're slouching.

妈妈的话是对的：如果你无精打采地站着，连腰都挺不直，就永远够不到星星。

Mom was right. You can't reach for the stars if you're slouching[1].

I remember thinking about a middle-aged man standing at an adjacent checkout counter. Something set him apart. Even the boy bagging groceries seemed to sense it. He did a speedier-than-usual job as he glanced with respect at the man.

Trying to pinpoint what was different about him, I found that he looked quite ordinary. Although he gave the impression of being tall, I could see he was actually a little shorter than average. His features weren't particularly outstanding, and he was wearing plain weekend sports attire.

Not until the man was leaving did it strike me. He carried himself as if he were somebody worth caring about, head up and chest out, he walked proudly from the market.

Suddenly, words I'd heard my mother repeat hundreds of times as I was growing up held new meaning. "Stand up straight! Lift yourself by pretending strings are pulling you from the tops of your ears."

I thought of myself being pulled up, and my head and upper torso[2] lifted automatically. I felt taller as I approached the market's doors. This time I saw reflected a woman who looked as if she knew where she was going! But I rushed home in five o'clock traffic and tried to fix dinner before a seven o'clock meeting, my

妈妈的话是对的：如果你无精打采地站着，连腰都挺不直，就永远够不到星星。

我想起一个站在紧挨着的付款台边上的中年男士，有一些东西使他显得与众不同。就连装杂货的小男孩好像都感觉到了。小男孩带着敬意看了那个男人一眼，干起活来都比平时快了。

我努力找出他的与众不同之处，但发现他看起来很普通。尽管他给人们的印象很高大，我可以看出来实际上他比一般人要矮一点儿。他没有十分明显的特征，他穿着很普通的周末穿的运动衣。

直到他离开时我才发现：他的姿态就好像他是一个值得关注的人，昂首挺胸，自豪地从市场中走了出去。

突然，成长过程中妈妈重复了几百次的话对我有了新的含义。“站直了！就像耳朵上拉着两根绳一样。”

我想着自己被拉直了，我的头和上身自然就挺起来了。走向超市的门时我觉得自己高了。这次我看见玻璃上映出一个似乎知道自己要走向哪儿去的女人！但我5点坐车跑回家，又尽力在7点开会前做好晚饭，优美的姿态消失得无影无踪。

❶ **slouch** /slaʊtʃ/
v. 无精打采地立、坐或走

❷ **torso** /ˈtɔːsəʊ/
n. 躯干

good posture vanished.

It wasn't until the next day as I was trying on clothes in a department store that I remembered again. Each thing I put on bulged[3], rippled and tucked in the wrong places. I turned sideways, thinking that perhaps from a different angle I'd look better. That's when I realized how really poor my posture was. Suddenly I recalled the man in the supermarket. Standing straight helped him look wonderfully attractive and special. Could it help me look better in these clothes?

I lifted myself up and anxiously looked at the dress again. Unattractive bulges and tucks had smoothed themselves out, and the lines were nicer. I liked the dress!

"Dynamite[4]!" said the clerk who was helping me.

"You like this?"

"Yes. It makes you look thinner too."

Sure enough, I looked five to seven pounds lighter. Dieting titles I'd read come to mind, such as "How to Lose Pounds in Weeks." Now I had a new title: "How to Look Thinner in Seconds."

Did I look younger, too, when I stood straight? I had to admit I probably did. Now I had another new title: "How to Look Years Younger in Seconds." And I began to notice that I didn't have the

直到第二天我在商店试衣服的时候才又想起来。我试的每件衣服都在不应该的地方鼓起来并起褶。我侧身照了照，想也许从一个不同的角度我会看起来好一些。那时我真正意识到我的姿态多么糟糕。突然我想起了超市中的那位男士，站得笔直使他看起来很具吸引力也十分特别。这样能不能让我穿着这些衣服也更好看些呢？

我站直了，急切地又照了一眼这件衣服。衣服凸起的地方和褶子自己都平了，线条也更好看了。我喜欢这件衣服！

“太好了！”为我服务的售货员说。

“你喜欢这件？”

“是的，它使你看起来更苗条。”

当然，我看起来轻了5至7磅。我立刻想起来我读过的一些有关控制饮食的文章的标题，比如“如何在几周内减轻几磅。”现在我有了一个新标题：“如何在几秒钟内看起来更苗条。”

当我站直了，也看起来更年轻了吗？我不得不承认也许是这样。现在我又有了一个新标题：“如何在几秒钟内看起来年轻几岁？”我开始注意到购物时我不再背疼了。在回家的车上，我肯定我其他方面也感觉更好了。我把新鲜空气直接吸入肺的底部并呼出

❸ **bulge** /bʌldʒ/ *v.* 鼓起，凸起

❹ **dynamite** /ˈdaɪnəmaɪt/ *n.* 了不起的人或事物

backache I usually get on shopping trips. In the car on the way home, I was sure I felt better in other ways. For one thing, I was breathing all the way down to the bottom of my lungs for a change. And my insides were all properly aligned[5] now instead of scrunching together. Then another title occurred to me: "How to feel Better in Seconds."

But it still didn't feel natural to stand up straight. Gravity and years of bad habit kept pulling me downward. Maybe that's why on the day of a party I had worried about, I lowered my head and slouched. I didn't want to go. I wasn't comfortable with that group, and I knew I'd say all the wrong things.

After dinner, as I reluctantly[6] put on my new dress, I caught a glimpse of myself in the mirror. "Stand up straight! " I ordered. I pretended strings were pulling me upward; I lifted myself to full height. And that's how I walked into that party.

I was surprised at what good posture did to change my appearance, but I was astonished at what it did to the rest of me — my spirits, my attitude, my feelings about myself. I imagine it happened like this: As I lifted my body to its full height and held up my head, little signals went to my brain saying, "You're confident. You think highly of yourself. You are somebody of worth." Other people, reacting to the way I looked, also sent signals — signals of respect. They must have thought: Well, if she thinks she's somebody of worth, she must be. I began feeling relaxed and I was able to be outgoing — much more so than usual. That

废气。我的内脏都在正确的位置上而不是挤在一起。然后我又想到了一个新标题："如何在几秒钟内感觉更好。"

但是站直了我仍感觉不自然。地球引力和这些年的坏习惯总使我站不直。也许这正是我为那天的晚会忧虑的原因，我低着头，无精打采地坐在那里。我不想去和那些人在一起，我不舒服，而且我知道我会说错所有的话。

晚饭后，当我不情愿地穿上新衣服时，我瞥了一眼镜子中的自己。"站直了！"我命令道。我假装有绳子向上拉我，站到最直，就这样去参加了晚会。

我惊奇于好的姿态给我的相貌带来的改变，更让我惊奇的是它对我的精神、态度和自我感觉的作用。我想它是这样发生的：当我站直了抬起头时，一些小信号传输给我的大脑，"你是自信的。你对自己评价很高。你是值得尊重的重要的人物。"其他人也对我的样子表示钦佩。他们肯定认为：噢，如果她认为她是个值得尊重的重要人物，她肯定是。我感到很放松，也比平时开朗多了。那晚当我上床睡觉时，我意识到我还有另一个新标题："如何在几秒钟内感到自信。"

接下来的几个星期，我发现长期保持优

❺ **align** /əˈlaɪn/
v. 安装到相互间正确的位置上

❻ **reluctantly** /rɪˈlʌktəntlɪ/
adv. 不情愿地，勉强的

night as I went to bed, I realized that I had still another new title: "How to Feel Confident in Seconds."

During the weeks since then, I have found that long-term good posture continues to help me. I feel more inclined to stand up for what I believe as I stand up physically. And standing taller, I feel better about myself. This helps me to be better, which, in turn, gives me greater peace and happiness inside.

The other day, while I was shopping, the checker looked at me as if she thought she knew me. "Say, aren't you somebody?" she asked me.

"Well, come to think of it, yes," I said, "I am somebody. Aren't we all?"

美的姿态继续对我有帮助。我觉得当我站直了的时候，我更愿意支持维护我相信的事物。站得越直，自我感觉越好。这使我更优秀，同时也给我内心带来了更大的平静与幸福。

不久前的一天，我买东西时，收款员看着我好像认识我一样。“喂，你不就是某个重要人物吗?”她问我。

“噢，想想，我就是，”我说，“我是个重要人物。我们不都是吗?”

Room for the future

未来大有可为

The loss of my job was responsible for some positive changes in my life. Revisiting the past made room for the future.

丢掉工作使我的生活得到了积极的改变。重访过去为未来打开了空间。

At the age of forty-five, my usually well-ordered life became fraught with changes.

After twenty-two years of working for a major financial institution, a downsizing initiative and a major bank merger resulted in the elimination of over one hundred jobs, mine being one of them.

My once secure future became a fallacy[1]. However, I was one of the lucky ones. I was not a single parent, not dependent solely on my income, but just like the other ex-bankers, I had become a disposable employee, and a statistician.

My mantra has always been "change is good, change is progress," but when it affected my livelihood, I had to revise it to "accept change and make the most of it." From the beginning, I chose to look at this occurrence not as a misfortune, but as a welcome opportunity. I refused to become depressed or bitter; instead, I eagerly anticipated doing something new and different.

Having a positive attitude made all the difference in the way I perceived the future. First, I decided to return to college and graduate, several decades later than I should have. Doing this at my age took more than a little courage. Not being a graduate had never held me back in my career with the bank, but now it was a personal goal I longed to achieve. With a little trepidation[2] and a lot of determination, I registered for evening classes, and became an adult student.

在45岁时，我的有条不紊的生活充满了变数。

我就职于一家重要的金融机构22年后，突然失去了工作，是一次裁员和一次重大的银行并购所导致的，100多名员工被裁，其中就有我。

我对未来的安全感烟消云散。然而，我还是幸运的。我不是单亲家长，薪水也不是唯一的收入来源，但是正像其他前银行职员一样，我成了一名可有可无的雇员，一名统计人员。

我的祷文一向是“变化是好的，变化是进步”，但当它影响我的生活时，我不得不将之改为“接受变化并善加利用”。从一开始，我就选择了把发生的一切看作是一个很好的开始，而不是一种不幸。我拒绝了沮丧、愤恨，取而代之的是我渴望尝试新的、不同于以往的事情。

拥有积极的态度使我对未来的看法完全改变了。首先，我决定重返校园并取得大学文凭，虽然已晚了几十年。这般年龄采取如此行动需要拿出些勇气。没有大学文凭并没有影响我在银行的职业生涯，但现在获得学位是我的目标。我有些忐忑不安，但决心很大，我在夜校报了名，成为了一名成人学生。

❶ **fallacy**
/ˈfæləsɪ/
n. 谬误，谬论
❷ **trepidation**
/ˌtrepɪˈdeɪʃn/
n. 惊恐，恐慌

Oral presentations were often required for one class. I remember thinking that if I had known this beforehand, I would have taken something else to achieve my required accreditation. By nature, I am a rather reticent[3] individual, and speaking in front of people terrified me. As I stood in front of the other adults with whom I shared a common goal, my knees were visibly knocking, and my heartbeat almost audible[4]. Somehow, I found my voice and squeaked out my presentation. The next time it was easier, and soon, I was starting to enjoy it a little. Later in the year, I even voluntarily interviewed a local reporter for an English assignment, much to the amazement of my teacher. My confidence level soared[5]. Suddenly I felt like I could accomplish anything.

During this time, I realized that no matter what life throws our way, personal growth never stops. It comes from within, and needs only to be challenged in order to surface. It is entirely possible to step out of one's comfort zone to learn something new. My experience of going back to school ended up being far more valuable than just acquiring a diploma.

The second thing I did to improve my inner self was to reevaluate my life. It used to be filled with endless, and sometimes meaningless, events. Now, instead of working towards materialistic things and personal glorification[6], my heart and life are firmly entwined[7] around people I care for.

Yes, having a fulfilling career is important, but it is no longer my reason for being. When I rejoin the "rat race", it will be on my

有一门课程常常要求学生进行口头陈述。记得我曾想，如果我事先知道这一要求，我会选择其他课程来挣够学分。我天性沉默寡言，在众人面前说话令我十分畏惧。当我站在其他和我有着共同目标的成人面前时，我的膝盖在打颤，心快跳到嗓子了。终于我勉强把陈述做完。第二次就容易多了，不久，我有一点喜欢这门课程了。那年，我竟主动为一项英语作业采访了当地的一位记者，这使我的老师惊叹不已。我的信心倍增。忽然我觉得我没有做不成的事。

在这期间，我意识到无论我们在人生道路上有什么遭遇，个人的成长是永无止境的。它是内在的需要，只有迎接挑战才能超越自我。跳出自己的“舒适圈”去学习新的东西是完全可能的。重返学校给我的收获很多，远远超过一张学位证书。

第二件完善自我的事情是重新评价了我的生活。我过去的生活尽是些没完没了的、无意义的事情。现在，我的身心与我所关心的人紧紧地连在一起，而不是为了物质财富和个人的荣誉而工作。

是的，事业有成是重要的，但它已不再是我生活的目标。如果我重返“激烈的竞争”，那将按照我的条件，因为我把滋养灵魂

❸ **reticent** /ˈretɪsnt/ *adj.* 沉默寡言的

❹ **audible** /ˈɔːdəbl/ *adj.* 听得见的

❺ **soar** /sɔː/ *vt.* 剧增，高飞

❻ **glorification** /ˌglɔːrɪfɪˈkeɪʃn/ *n.* 赞颂

❼ **entwine** /ɪnˈtwaɪn/ *v.* (使)缠住，(使)盘绕

terms, as nurturing[8] my soul is my first priority. Having simplified my life, I am enjoying living now, instead of just existing to make a living.

Is there life after banking? You bet there is.

The loss of my job was responsible for some positive changes in my life. Revisiting the past made room for the future. As I contemplate the meaning of my mantra[9] "change is good, change is progress", I realize that I have accepted the change, and am making the most of it.

And, I have only just begun. The best is yet to come.

视为第一重要。将生活简化，我是在享受生活，而不是为了生计而生存。

银行生涯之后还有生活吗？当然有。

丢掉工作使我的生活得到了积极的改变。重访过去为未来打开了空间。当我细细琢磨我的祷文“变化是好事，变化是进步”时，我意识到我已经接受了变化，并在充分利用它。

而且这只是个开始，精彩的还在后头。

❽ **nurture**
/ˈnɜːtʃə/
vt. 滋养，养育，给予营养

❾ **mantra**
/ˈmæntrə/
n. 祷文

The dreamer

梦想家

At the top of one wall she stenciled, The world always makes way for the dreamer.

在一面墙的顶部，她印上了这样一句话：世界总是为梦想者让路。

When I was nine years old living in a small town in North Carolina I found an ad for selling greeting cards in the back of a children's magazine. I thought to myself I can do this.I begged my mother to let me send for the kit.

Two weeks later when the kit arrived, I ripped off the brown paper wrapper[1], grabbed the cards and dashed from the house.

Three hours later, I returned home with no card and a pocket full of money proclaiming[2], "Mama, all the people couldn't wait to buy my cards! "A sales person was born. When I was twelve years old, my father took me to see Zig Ziegler. I remember sitting in that dark auditorium[3] listening to Mr.Zigler raise everyone's spirits up to the ceiling. I left there feeling like I could do anything.

When we got to the car, I turned to my father and said, "Dad, I want to make people feel like that."

My father asked me what I meant.

"I want to be a motivational speaker just like Mr.Ziegler," I replied. A dream was born. Recently, began pursuing my dream of motivating others. After a four-year relationship with a major fortune 100 company beginning as a sales trainer and ending as a regional sales manager, I left the company at the height of my career. Many people were astounded that I would leave after earning a six-figure income. And they asked why I would risk everything for a dream.

我9岁的时候，住在加利福尼亚北部的一个小镇上，我在一本儿童杂志的背面发现一则卖贺卡的广告。我认为我可以做这项工作。我请求妈妈让我要一套。

两周过后，我拿到贺卡了，撕掉棕色的包装纸，抓起贺卡冲出了家门。

三小时后，我回到家。一张贺卡都没剩下，带着满口袋的钱宣布："妈妈，所有的人都等不及要买我的贺卡！"一个销售人才就这样诞生了。我12岁的时候，爸爸带我去听齐格勒的演讲。我记得坐在黑压压的观众席上，听到齐格勒先生把每个人的士气都提升到几乎要冲破屋顶。我离开那里，感觉好像我可以做所有的事情。

当我们上了车，我转向爸爸说："爸爸，我也想使人们有那样的感觉。"

我爸爸问我是什么意思。

"我想做一个像齐格勒先生一样的鼓舞人的演讲家，"我回答。一个梦想出现了。近来，我开始追求给别人动力的梦想。我在一家大公司开始做销售培训员，后来做到地区销售经理，我在这里工作4年后，在职业生涯处于顶峰时我离开了。我竟然在得到6位数字的收入后离开了，这使许多人感到惊奇，他们问为什么我为一个梦想冒牺牲一切的危

❶ **wrapper**
/ˈræpə/
n. 包装材料

❷ **proclaim**
/prəˈkleɪm/
v. 宣告，公布，声明

❸ **auditorium**
/ˌɔːdɪˈtɔːrɪəm/
n. 观众席，听众席

I made my decision to start my own company and leave my secure position after attending a regional sales meeting. The vice-president of our company delivered a speech that changed my life. He asked us, "If a genie[4] would grant[5] you three wishes, what would they be? " After giving us a moment to write down the three wishes, he then asked us, "Why do you need a genie? "I would never forget the empowerment I felt at that moment. I realized that everything I had accomplished, the graduate degree, the successful sales career, speaking engagements, training and managing for a fortune 100 company had prepared me for this moment.

I was ready and did not need a genie's help to become a motivational speaker. When I tearfully told my boss my plans this incredible leader whom I respect so much replied, "Precede with reckless[6] abandon and you will be successful."

Having made that decision, I was immediately tested. One week after I gave notice[7], my husband was laid off from his job.

We had recently bought a new home and needed both incomes to make the monthly mortgage payment and now we were done to no income. It was tempting to turn back to my former company, knowing they wanted me to stay but I was certain that if I went back, I would never leave. I decided I still wanted to move forward rather than end up with a mouth full of "if only" later on. A motivational speaker was born. When I held fast to my dream, even during the tough times, the miracles really began to happen.

险。

参加一个地区销售会议之后，我决定离开稳定的职位去开创属于我自己的公司。我们公司的副总经理做了一个改变我一生的演讲。他问我们："如果有个神答应帮助你实现三个愿望，它们会是什么？"给我们一段时间写下这三个愿望之后，他问我们："你们为什么需要神呢？"我永远也忘不了那时那刻我所感受到的鼓舞。我意识到我所完成的每件事：研究生学历，成功的销售生涯，从事演讲工作，在公司做培训和管理，都为这个时刻作好了准备。

我已经整装待发并且不需要神的帮助来成为一名给人动力的演讲者了。当我含着泪把我的计划告诉老板时，这个我十分崇敬的令人难以相信的领导说："甩开膀子往前撞，你会成功的。"

做了那个决定后，我很快受到了考验。我交辞职报告一周后，丈夫就下岗了。

我们最近刚买了一套新房，需要我们俩每月的收入来还贷款，现在我们都没收入了。回到以前的公司诱惑力很大，我知道他们想让我留下来，但是我十分清楚如果我回去了，我就永远离不开了。我决定我仍然要继续前进，而不是以后张口闭口都说"要是……该

❹ **genie** /ˈdʒiːnɪ/ *n.* 神怪

❺ **grant** /ɡrɑːnt/ *v.* 同意给予或答应所求

❻ **reckless** /ˈreklɪs/ *adj.* 不考虑后果的，不顾危险的

❼ **notice** /ˈnəʊtɪs/ *n.* 辞职报告

In a short time period my husband found a better job.We didn't miss a mortgage payment.And I was able to book several speaking engagements with new clients. I discovered the incredible power of dreams.

I loved my old job, my peers and the company I left, but it was time to get on with my dream. To celebrate my success I had a local artist paint my new office as a garden. At the top of one wall she stenciled[8], "The world always makes way for the dreamer."

多好”来结束我的梦想。一个给人动力的演讲家诞生了。当我抓紧我的梦想时，甚至在最艰难的时期，奇迹真的发生了。

在很短的时间内，我丈夫找到了一份更好的工作。我们没耽误还贷款。我也可以和新客户签几个演讲协议。我发现了梦想神奇的力量。

我热爱我以前的工作，我的同事还有我离开的那家公司，但是到了该追求我自己的梦想的时候了。为了庆祝我的成功，我让一位地方的画家把我的新办公室用油漆喷成了花园的样子。在一面墙的顶部，她印上了这样一句话：世界总是为梦想者让路。

❽ **stencil**
/ˈstensl/
v. 用墨板或蜡纸印刷图案、文字等

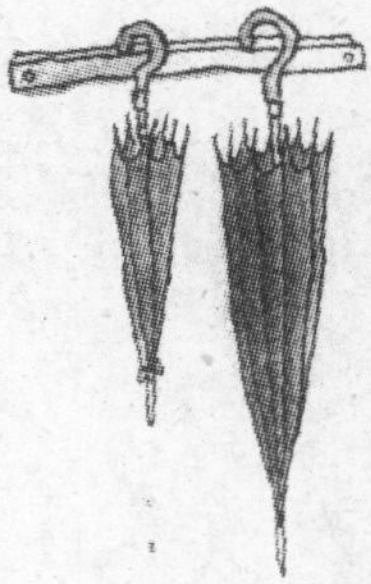

Take charge of your day

安排时间

Remember, the best time to plant a tree was 20 years ago. The second best time is now.

记住，种树的最佳时间是20年前，仅次于它的最好时间就是现在。

People occasionally tell you, "Do that in your free time," but in fact there's no such thing as "free" time. Even when you're lying by the swimming pool, that's leisure time — but it isn't free time.

To prove that all time has value, a senior executive at a large corporation[1] in the Northeast asked everyone who attended a meeting to "punch[2] in." At the session's end he calculated the total price of the meeting in manhours and converted[3] these into dollars by prorating each staffer's salary. Indeed, for each $10,000 you make annually, a single hour is worth $5. And if you can save just one hour a day, you'll not only conserve[4] thousands of dollars' worth of time each year but also give yourself opportunities to learn and do things that make your time even more valuable. That's why the most successful people are those who've mastered the time-saving tactics described here.

Stay Focused

All top performers establish priorities. Helen Gurley Brown, editor-in-chief of *Cosmopolitan*, always keeps an issue of the magazine on her desk. Whenever she's tempted to fritter[5] away time, doing something that doesn't contribute to the magazine's success, she glances at that issue, and it gets her back on track.

Pattern of Success

Most people who want to get ahead spend useful time writing personal notes of gratitude[6], sympathy and congratulations. But when it comes to routine memos[7], letters, fact sheets and forms, they save a lot of time by relying on previously written material.

人们有时候会对你说:“在你空闲的时候做那件事吧”,但是,实际上这种“空闲”时间是没有的。即使当你躺在游泳池边时,那也是休闲时间,而非空闲时间。

为了证明所有的时间都有价值,(美国)东北部一家大公司的一位高级管理人员要求每个参加会议的人来开会时都要“打卡”签到。在会议结束时,他计算出这次会议占用的工时的总数,再根据每位职员的薪金按比例地将它转换成美元。的确,对于一个一年挣1万美元的人来说,1小时就价值5美元。那么,如果你一天能节省1小时,一年下来,你就不仅节约了价值几千美元的时间,而且还给自己提供了许多机会去学习和做那些使你的时间更有价值的事情。因此,大多数成功者掌握了以下几种节约时间的方法。

专心致志

所有获得成功的人做事都分主次。《大都市》月刊的主编海伦·格利·布朗总是在办公桌上放一本自己办的杂志。每当她受到什么事情引诱而消磨时间、做一些与杂志成功无关的事情时,看看那本杂志,她的注意力就会回到正事上来。

成功的模式

大多数想获得成功的人都利用有用的时

❶ **corporation** /ˌkɔːpəˈreɪʃn/ *n.* 公司,法人团体

❷ **punch** /pʌntʃ/ *v.* 打(孔),给某物穿孔

❸ **convert** /kənˈvɜːt/ *v.* 改变(某事物)的形式或用途

❹ **conserve** /kənˈsɜːv/ *v.* 保存,保护

❺ **fritter** /ˈfrɪtə/ *v.* 愚蠢地浪费

❻ **gratitude** /ˈgrætɪtjuːd/ *n.* 感激,感谢

❼ **memo** /ˈmeməʊ/ *n.* 备忘录

Susan Taylor, editor-in-chief of *Essence*, has created some 40 form letters for everything from article rejections to replies to requests for donations. Stored on her computer, the letters can be called up, copied and customized by changing a few key words. Taylor then often adds a handwritten greeting at the bottom as a personal touch.

Telephone Tips

Financier J. B. Fuqua has made a fortune putting deals together over the telephone. His most important strategy is to make notes before he places a call.

To avoid playing telephone tag[8], return phone calls right away, because you're likely to catch the caller and your messages won't pile up. If the person is busy, many time-tacticians make an appointment to call back. Leaving a detailed message on someone's voice mail prevents you from getting tied up in long conversations and will get you an answer more quickly.

Do It Now

As a renowned color consultant, the late Suzanne Caygill designed the homes and wardrobes[9] of celebrities. To deal with all the demands of her schedule, she followed a rule learned from her seam-stress grandmother: If she had a job to do, she did it immediately. Too many people waste time "commencing to proceed to get started," Caygill would say.

If you just dive in, though, you'll be surprised at how fast you

间来写表示感谢、慰问和祝贺的私人信函。但是，如果所要写的是日常工作的备忘录、公函、资料汇总和表格的话，他们就会依靠以前写过的文字资料来节省大量时间。

《精粹》杂志的主编苏珊·泰勒起草了大约40种复信格式，从退稿到答复捐赠请求，样样俱备。这些信都储存在电脑中，可以随时调出、复制，只要改动几个关键的字词就成了一份专门写给某人的信件了。之后，泰勒常常会在信的结尾处加上一句亲笔写的问候语，以示亲切。

打电话须知

金融家J·B·富卡通过电话集中做生意，发了大财。他最重要的策略是在打电话之前把要说的话写下来。

为了避免打电话时找不到人而玩捉迷藏，要及时给别人回电话，因为你很容易找到打电话的人，这样你的留言就不会堆积起来。如果那个人此时正忙，许多善于运用时间的人就会约个时间再回电话。在有些人的录音电话中留下详细的口信，可以使你免受长时间谈话之累，还会使你更快地得到答复。

现在就做

作为一名著名的色彩顾问，苏珊娜·凯吉尔生前曾为许多知名人士设计房间和个人服

❽ **tag** /tæg/
n. （儿童的）捉人游戏

❾ **wardrobe** /ˈwɔːdrəʊb/
n. （个人的）全部衣服

get things done. Remember, the best time to plant a tree was 20 years ago. The second best time is now.

Freeze the Design

Perfectionists can waste just as much time as procrastinators[10]. Thomas R. Williams, former chairman of Wachovia Corporation, discovered that many young people in banking don't know when to stop researching a project and start wrapping it up. Those trainees could have learned something from engineers, who are taught to produce the best possible solution by a certain date. Even if a design is not perfect, they've done the best they could under deadline.

装。为了应付她时间表上的各种事情，她依照一条从她祖母那里学来的原则：如果有什么工作要做，她立即就做。凯吉尔说，很多人把时间浪费在“准备工作”上。

尽管你刚刚开始这么做事，但是你也会对自己这么快就做完了事情感到意外。记住，种树的最佳时间是20年前，仅次于它的最好时间就是现在。

冻结方案

追求完美的人与那些爱拖延的人浪费的时间一样多。瓦霍维娅公司前董事长托马斯·R·威廉斯发现，许多在银行界工作的年轻人不知道什么时候该停止研究方案，什么时候该着手结束工作。那些接受培训的人倒应该向工程师学习一些东西，工程师们懂得，他们应在某一日期前拿出可能的最佳方案。即使方案不那么完美，但是他们已经在规定的期限内做了最大的努力。

⑩ **procrastinator** /prəʊˈkræstɪneɪtə/ *n.* 爱拖延时间的人

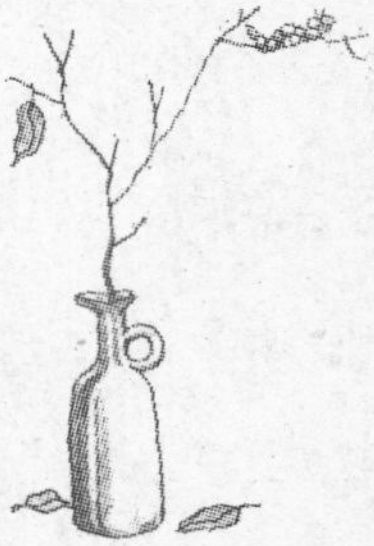

Truths to live by

赖以生存的真理

I remembered how often I, too, had been indifferent to the grandeur of each day, too preoccupied with petty and sometimes even mean concerns to respond to the splendor of it all.

我想起自己也经常对每一天的伟大视而不见，因为一些小事心事重重，有时甚至对每天的壮观不做任何反应。

The art of living is to know when to hold fast and when to let go. For life is a paradox: it enjoins[1] us to cling to its many gifts even while it ordains[2] their eventual relinquishment[3]. The rabbis[4] of old put it this way: "A man comes into this world with his fist clenched, but when he dies, his hand is open."

Surely we ought to hold fast to life, for it is wondrous, and full of a beauty that breaks through every pore of God's own earth. We know that this is so, but all too often we recognize this truth only in our backward glance when we remember with far greater pain that we did not see that beauty when it flowered, that we failed to respond with love to love when it was tendered.

A recent experience re-taught me this truth. I was hospitalized following a severe heart attack and had been in intensive care for several days. It was not a pleasant place.

One morning, I had to have some additional tests. The required machines were located in a building at the opposite end of the hospital, so I had to be wheeled across the courtyard.

As we emerged from our unit, the sunlight hit me. That's all there was to my experience. Just the light of the sun. And yet how beautiful it was — how warming how sparkling, how brilliant!

I looked to see whether anyone else relished the sun's golden glow, but everyone was hurrying to and fro, most with their eyes fixed on the ground. Then I remembered how often I, too,

生活的艺术在于知道什么时候该抓紧，什么时候该放开。因为生活是矛盾的：当生活命令我们永远放弃某事物时，又让我们紧拥它的许多馈赠。古代的拉比这样解释：“人来到这个世界上时，拳头是紧握着的，但当他死去时，手是张开的。”

当然我们应该抓紧生命，因为它很精彩，充满美好，而且这些美好超过了上帝自己的土地上所有的一切。我们知道这些，但常常只有当我们回过头看时才会认识这条真理，我们为没看到花开时的美丽难受，没能用爱回应别人给予的爱而悲伤。

最近的一段经历再次教会了我这条真理。我由于严重的心脏病住进了医院，而且在特重监护区待了几天。它可不是一个让人愉快的地方。

一天早晨，我需要做一些额外的检查。因为检查用的仪器在医院的另一头，所以我坐在轮椅上被推着穿过这个院子。

当我们到检查的地方时，阳光射到了我身上。我觉得所有的美好都在这里，只说太阳的光芒，它多么漂亮，多么温暖，多么明亮，多么灿烂啊！

我注意看了看是否还有其他人也珍惜这金色的阳光，但所有人都匆忙地来来往往，

❶ **enjoin**
/ɪnˈdʒɔɪn/
v. 将（行动或禁令）强施于某人，命令

❷ **ordain**
/ɔːˈdeɪn/
v. 命令，规定，注定

❸ **relinquishment**
/rɪˈlɪŋkwɪʃmənt/
n. 放弃，松手放开

❹ **rabbi**
/ˈræbaɪ/
n. 拉比（犹太教教士及其头衔，犹太教法学导师）

had been indifferent to the grandeur[5] of each day, too preoccupied[6] with petty and sometimes even mean concerns to respond to the splendor of it all.

The insight gleaned[7] from that experience is really as commonplace as was the experience itself: life's gifts are precious-but we are too heedless of them.

Here then is the first pole of life's paradoxical demands on us: Never be too busy for the wonder and the awe of life. Be reverent[8] before each dawning day. Embrace each hour. Seize each golden minute.

Hold fast to life... but not so fast that you cannot let go. This is the second side of life's coin, the opposite pole of its paradox: we must accept our losses, and learn how to let go.

This is not an easy lesson to learn, especially when we are young and think that the world is ours to command, that whatever we desire with the full force of our passionate being can, may will, be ours. But then life moves along to confront us with realities, and slowly but surely this second truth dawns upon us.

大多数人眼睛都盯着地。然后我想起自己也经常对每一天的伟大视而不见，因为一些小事心事重重，有时甚至对每天的壮观不做任何反应。

通过这件事得到的启示实际上和这件事本身一样普通：生活的给予是珍贵的，但是我们太不注意它们了。

这是生活对我们要求的一端，它看似矛盾：不要忙碌得顾不上生活的美好和阴暗。崇敬每一天，拥抱每一小时，抓紧宝贵的每一分钟。

抓紧生命…但也不要太紧以至于你放不下。这是生活这枚硬币的另一面，即矛盾的另一端：我们必须接受失去，学习如何放开。

这可并不简单，尤其当我们还年轻，认为世界应该由我们自己掌握时，希望我们完全控制自己的情感。但随着生命的前进，我们必须面对现实，渐渐的我们肯定会明白第二条真理。

❺ **grandeur** /ˈgrændʒə/ *n.* 伟大，壮丽，壮观

❻ **preoccupied** /priːˈɒkjʊpaɪd/ *n.* 心不在焉的，心事重重的

❼ **glean** /gliːn/ *v.* 搜集

❽ **reverent** /ˈrevərənt/ *adj.* 虔诚的，恭敬的

Don't fear failure

不要害怕失败

You learn a great deal more from what doesn't work than from what does.

你会从未成功的事中比成功的事中学到更多的东西。

Many career experts tout[1] failure as the castor oil of success. The idea isn't to fling yourself into certain disaster in order to be mystically rewarded with triumph. Rather, it's a simple recognition that people who willingly risk failure and learn from loss have the best chance of succeeding at whatever they try.

If you haven't crashed, you may be in snooze[2] mode, coasting[3] and taking too few risks to be challenged. Oh, you've had minor reverses[4] in school or love, but you haven't failed meaningfully. Never fear, says Amitai Etzioni, professor of socio-economics at George Washington University: "Everyone gets a chance. No one lives a failure-proof life forever."

Failure is easy to recognize. "It usually involves loss of money, self-esteem or status," says Carole Hyatt, co-author of *When Smart People Fail.* At the very least, it is simply not getting what you want.

Not that rational people should wish for calamity[5], says Rabbi Harold Kushner, author of *When Bad Things Happen to Good People.* But a stiff dose of misfortune is often a painfully effective tutor. It "teaches you something about your strength and acquaints you with your limitations," notes Kushner. "That's an important part of maturity."

People who profit from loss are the kind of foot soldiers business leaders seek, "Continuous success builds arrogance and complacency[6]," says multibillionaire industrialist H. Ross Perot. "I want

许多职业专家把失败高度评价为成功的润滑油。这个想法不是为了把你先推向灾难然后再奇妙地使你起死回生获得成功，而只是认识到愿意冒失败的风险，从失败中学习的人无论尝试什么都最有可能成功。

如果你还没有崩溃，你可能处于睡眠状态，不费力就能取得进展，而且很少有风险的挑战。噢，你可能在学校或爱情上有些小的不幸，但你没有有意义地失败过。Amitai Etzioni，乔治华盛顿大学社会经济学教授，说，永远别害怕："每个人都有一个机会，没有人注定一生永远失败。"

失败很容易被认出来。《当聪明的人失败时》这一书的作者 Carole Hyatt 说："它通常包括金钱、自尊或地位的损失，"至少，它只是指没有得到你想要的。

并不是说理智的人应该盼望灾难，《当不幸的事发生在好人身上时》的作者 Robbi Harold Kusher 说，虽然严重的挫折通常是令人悲伤的，但又是有效的指导。它告诉你，"你的长处并且让你了解你的短处"，Kusher 写道，"那是成熟的代价。"

从失败中获益的人是公司领导所寻找的，"不断的成功建造了傲慢和自满，"拥有亿万财富的工业家 H·Ross Perot 说，"我想要那

❶ **tout** /taʊt/
v. 卖高价票

❷ **snooze** /snuːz/
n. 小睡，午睡

❸ **coast** /kəʊst/
v. 不费力而取得进展

❹ **reverse** /rɪˈvɜːs/
n. 不幸

❺ **calamity** /kəlˈæmətɪ/
n. 灾难

❻ **complacency** /kəmˈpleɪsnsɪ/
n. 自满

people who love the battlefield, people willing to go to the war". That includes making honest mistakes. Unsuccessful people, he adds, instinctively avoid risks even when a smart gamble might pay off. "You learn a great deal more from what doesn't work than from what does." Failure, he says, is merely the cost of seeking new challenge.

If the thought of fouling up paralyzes you, here are several helpful suggestions:

1. *Stop using the "F" word.* High achievers, rarely refer to "failure," a loaded word suggesting a personal dead end. They prefer "glitch," "bollix" or "course correction."

2. *Don't take it personally*[7]. When things go sour, do you instinctively label yourself a loser? The language you use to describe yourself can become a powerful reality. Repeatedly calling yourself an unemployed salesperson not only labels you as out of work — synonymous with failure in our society — it considers yourself someone "with options". Those opinions include taking classes to develop new skills or bravely striking out on another career.

3. *Be prepared.* Help insulate yourself by mapping a catastrophe[8] plan. Ask yourself: What is the worst that can happen? Imagining loss of job or spouse can force you to clearly consider practical alternatives. Do you have enough insurance and cash reserves to carry you through a difficult period? Do you have tal

些喜欢战场，愿意去打仗的人。”这包括犯诚实的错误。他又说，不成功的人本能地避免冒险，甚至在当一场形势看好的赌博就要赢时也不敢冒险。“你会从未成功的事中比成功的事中学到更多的东西。”他说，失败只是寻求新的挑战的代价。

如果失败的想法使你不能前进，这里有几条有用的建议：

1.*停止使用“失败”这个词*。高成就者很少用“失败”这个词，这个含义颇多的词表明这个人无法继续发展。他们喜欢用“差错”“混乱”或者“改正的过程。”

2. *不要因失败而不高兴*。当事情变糟时，你是本能地把自己当作失败者吗？你用来形容自己的语言会变成强有力的现实。总称呼你自己是一个没被雇佣的推销员不仅标志你没有工作——而且也表示你在社会上的失败——它把你看作“可以选择的人”。这些选择包括参加学习班培养新技巧以及勇敢地在另一个职业中闯荡。

3. *做好准备*。通过规划一个灾难计划来帮助你自己免受不良因素影响。问你自己：最坏会发生什么？想象失去了工作或另一半可以强迫你仔细想想其他实际的选择。你有足够的保险或预留了足够现金可以使你渡过

❼ **take sth. personally**
为某事所触怒

❽ **catastrophe**
/kəˈtæstrəfɪ/
n. 突如其来的大灾难

ents that could bring in an income if your employer handed you a pink slip? Keep in mind that the Chinese ideogram[9] for "crisis" consists of the characters for both "danger" and "opportunity."

4. *Learn to fail intelligently.* Jack Matson, a University of Houston professor, developed a course his students dubbed[10] "Failure 101." Matson had his class build ice-cream-stick mock-ups of products no one would buy. "They designed hamster[11] hot tubs and kites to fly in hurricanes," says Matson.

The ideas were ridiculous, but once Matson's students equated failure with innovation instead of defeat, they felt free to try anything. Since most students had at least five failures before finding their business niche, they learned not to take failure as the last word, says Matson. "They learned to reload and get ready to shoot again."

5. *Nevre say die.* Early's Harrisonburg, construction company went belly up in 1975. Then only 25, Early borrowed on his home rather than declare bankruptcy. He continued to work in construction, trying to master the intricacies[12] of management. In 1982, he "got nervy[13] enough" to borrow more to start his own business again, having built a solid reputation with banks for getting through difficult times.

Early expanded his new construction business cautiously. He took college courses in business administration. By 1988, Early's company made *Inc.* magazine's list of the 500 fastest-growing

困难时期吗？如果你的老板解雇了你，你有可以带来收入的才华吗？记住汉字中“危机”这个词有由两个字组成的，代表“危险”和“机会”。

4. *学会聪明地失败。* Jack Maston，休斯敦一所大学的教授，开了一门被学生叫做“失败 101”的课。Maston 让他班里的学生制造没人会买的冰激凌棒模型。“他们设计像仓鼠似的热容器和在飓风中放的风筝，”Maston 说。

想法很荒唐，可是一旦 Maston 的学生把失败看作创新而不是挫折时，他们就会勇于尝试任何事。因为大多数学生在成功之前都至少失败了 5 次，所以他们学会了不把失败作为结局，Maston 说。“他们学会了换一条路来走，并准备好再次行动。”

5. *永远不放弃。* 厄尔利的 Harrisonburg 建筑公司 1975 年破产了。厄尔利那时才 25 岁，他向家里借钱并且没有宣布破产。他继续在建筑业工作，努力掌握有关管理的错综复杂的关系。1982 年，他“厚着脸皮”又借了更多的钱再次开始了他自己的生意，因为渡过了困难时期，他给银行留下了很好的口碑。

厄尔利谨慎地扩大了他的新建筑公司。

⑨ **ideogram** /ˈɪdɪəgræm/ *n.* 表意文字

⑩ **dub** /dʌb/ *v.* 起外号

⑪ **hamster** /ˈhæmstə/ *n.* 仓鼠

⑫ **intricacy** /ˈɪntrɪkəsɪ/ *n.* 错综复杂

⑬ **nervy** /ˈnɜːvɪ/ *adj.* 厚脸皮的

privately owned companies.

Early is not complacent. Memories of hard times haunt[14] him. "I can't afford to get arrogant about success," he says. "So I'm always trying to improve my business."

他参加了大学商业管理的课程。到1988年，厄尔利的公司成了INC.杂志的500个发展最快的私企之一。

厄尔利并不自满。他时常想起那段艰难的日子。“我负担不起对成功的傲慢，”他说，“所以我总是尽力发展我的生意”。

⑭ **haunt**
/hɔːnt/
v. 经常浮现于脑际

What successful people have in common

成功人士的共性

Today his expertise earns him a six-figure salary.

今天他的专业知识为他赢得了 6 位数字的年薪。

Is there a "success personality" — some winning combination of traits[1] that leads almost inevitably to achievement? If so, exactly what is that secret success formula, and can anyone cultivate it?

At the Gallup Organization we recently focused in depth on success, probing the attitudes and traits of 1500 prominent[2] people selected at random from *Who's Who* in America. The main criterion for inclusion in *Who's Who* is not wealth or social position, but current achievement in a given field. Our research pinpoints a number of traits that recur regularly among top achievers. Here are five of the most important:

1. *Common sense.* This is the most prevalent quality possessed by our respondents. Seventy-nine percent award themselves a top score in this category. And 61 percent say that common sense was very important in contributing to their success.

To most, common sense means the ability to render sound, practical judgments on everyday affairs. To do this, one has to sweep aside extraneous[3] ideas and get right to the core of what matters. A Texas oil and gas magnate[4] puts it this way: "The key ability for success is simplifying. In conducting meetings and dealing with industry regulators, reducing a complex problem to the simplest terms is highly important."

Is common sense a trait a person is born with, or can you do something to increase it? The oil man's answer is that common sense can definitely be developed. He attributes his to learning

有“成功的性格”吗？——即那些使人注定成功的优势组合。如果有，确切一些，成功的秘密是什么？每个人都可以走上成功之路吗？

在盖洛普组织，我们近来深入地集中研究了成功问题，在美国《名人录》中随机选择了1 500名杰出人物研究他们的态度和性格特征。在《名人录》中选择人物的重要标准不是财富和社会地位，而是他们在所属领域做出的被普遍接受的贡献。我们的研究准确地显示出，在较高成就者身上不断出现的几种性格特征。这里是5条最重要的：

1. *判断力*。这是我们的被调查者拥有的最普遍的品质。79%的人在这一项上都打了很高的分数。并且61%的人说判断力为他们的成功做出了重大贡献。

对大多数人来说，判断力指可以对日常事情做出合理的、符合实际的判断的能力。做到这一点，人们要排除与正题无关的思想，直接找到事情的核心。一名德克萨斯的石油和天然气业的巨头这样说：“成功的主要能力是简单化。在主持会议以及处理工业规定时，把一个复杂的问题变成最简单的条款是十分必要的。”

判断力是一个人天生的特征，还是后天

❶ **trait** /treɪt/
n. 特点

❷ **prominent** /ˈprɒmɪnənt/
adj. 杰出的，卓越的

❸ **extraneous** /ɪkˈstreɪnɪəs/
adj. 与正题无关的

❹ **magnate** /ˈmæɡneɪt/
n. 有才有势的地主或工业家

how to debate in school. Another way to increase your store of common sense is to observe it in others, learning from their — and your own — mistakes.

2. *Knowing one's field.* After common sense, specialized knowledge in one's field is the second most common trait possessed by the respondents, with three-fourths giving themselves an A in this category.

Geologist[5] Philip Oxley, former president of Tenneco Oil Exploration and Production Co. and now chairman of Tenneco Europe, attributes his success to having worked in the oil fields, by "sitting on wells and bird-dogging seismic crews," he learned the tricks of the trade firsthand. "People, who are going to be good managers need to have a practical understanding of the crafts in their business," he says. Today his expertise[6] earns him a six-figure salary.

On-the-job experience convinced people the importance of specialized knowledge. He says that "understanding why my equipment performs the way it does" is part of his success formula. A noteworthy[7] point: he obtained his specialized knowledge through self-education and not through formal schooling.

3. *Self-reliance.* Top achievers rely primarily on their own resources and abilities. Seventy-seven percent give themselves an A rating for this trait.

通过做一些事情来提高的呢？那位石油大亨的回答是判断力是肯定可以培养起来的。他把他的判断力归功于在学校学习如何辩论。另一种增加你常识的方法是观察别人，从别人和你自己的错误中学习。

2. *熟知你的领域*。在判断力之后，一个领域的专业知识是被调查者的第二个普遍特征，3/4 的人在这项上给他们自己打了 A。

地质学家飞利浦·奥克斯斯勒曾任 Tenneco 石油勘探公司的总裁，现在是 Tenneco 公司欧洲分公司的主席。他把自己的成功归结为曾在油田工作过，通过“坐在油井边，观察地震队的队员，”他学到了第一手的成功诀窍。“想要成为好的管理者的人需要对他生意所在的行业有实际的了解，”他说。今天他的专业知识为他赢得了 6 位数字的年薪。

实际工作的经验向人们证明了专业知识的重要性。他说“了解我的设备的工作方式”是他成功的秘密的一部分。值得注意的一点是：他是通过自学而不是正规的学校教育获得专业知识的。

3. *依靠自己*。出色的成功者主要依靠他们自己的资源和能力。77%的人给他们的这个特点打了 A。

❺ **geologist**
/dʒɪˈɒlədʒɪst/
n. 地质学研究者或专家

❻ **expertise**
/ˌekspɜːˈtiːz/
n. 专业知识或技能

❼ **noteworthy**
/ˈnəʊtˈwɜːθɪ/
adj. 值得注意的，显著的

Self-reliance is not how you feel or how good you are; rather, it's whether you have the gumption[8] to take definitive action to get things moving in your life. It includes plain old willpower and the ability to get goals.

Two-thirds of the respondents say they've had clear goals for their lives and careers. And half of those we interviewed give themselves an A in willpower. Among other capabilities, willpower encompasses the ability to be a self-starter and to persevere after a project has begun.

4. *General intelligence.* This is essential for outstanding achievement because it involves your natural ability to comprehend difficult concepts quickly and to analyze them clearly and incisively[9]. At least that's the way our respondents see it — 43 percent said it was a very important ingredient of their success, and another 52 percent said it was fairly important.

5. *Ability to get things done.* Nearly three-fourths of our high achievers rank themselves "very efficient" in accomplish tasks. And they agree that at least three important qualities have helped them to do so: organizational ability, good work habits and diligence.

A physics professor summarizes his success formula this way: "Sheer hard, tenacious work, with the ability to pace oneself." He admits working up to 100 hours a week.

依靠自己并不是你感觉如何或你有多好；而是你是否有魄力采取明确的行动从而在你的生活中启动这些事。它包括十分熟悉的意志力和达到目标的能力。

2/3 的被调查者说他们曾有明确的生活和职业目标。其中一半的人在意志力方面给自己打 A。在其他能力中，意志力包括主动开始一个项目并且坚持到底的能力。

4. *一般智能*。这一点是取得杰出成就必不可少的，因为它包括迅速理解困难的概念并能明了、精确地分析它们的能力。至少我们的被调查者是这么认为的——43%的人说这是他们成功的一个重要因素，另外 52%的人说它相当重要。

5. *完成事情的能力*。几乎 3/4 的高成就者认为他们在完成任务方面"十分有能力"。他们一致认为至少有三个重要的品质帮他们能够这么做：组织能力，好的工作习惯和勤奋。

一位物理学教授这样总结他的成功模式："百分百的努力，抓紧工作和使自己有规律匀速前进的能力。"他承认一周工作到过 100 个小时。

除了这里列出的 5 条外，还有其他一些影响成功的因素：领导能力，创造力，与他

❽ **gumption**
/ˈɡʌmpʃn/
n. 进取精神，魄力

❾ **incisively**
/ɪnˈsaɪsɪvlɪ/
adv. 清晰而精确地，直接地

Besides the five listed here, there are other factors that influence success: leadership, creativity, relationships with others, and, of course, luck. But common sense, knowing your field, self-reliance, intelligence and the ability to get things done stand out[10]. If you cultivate these traits, chances are you'll succeed. And you might even find yourself listed in *Who's Who* someday.

人的关系，当然还有运气。但是判断力、熟知你的领域、依靠自己、智能和完成事情的能力这5项比较突出。如果你培养这些特点，你就有机会成功。甚至某一天你会发现自己被列在《名人录》中。

⑩ **stand out**
突出，显眼

Save money for college by my own

自己挣钱读大学

Whenever I am overwhelmed or afraid of the future, I can remember my $64,268 miracle.

每当我对未来感到不知所措或惧怕时，我就会想到我那64,268美元的奇迹。

I will never forget one day in my first year in high school. I was sitting on the stairs descending[1] into the basement, putting my head in my hands and crying out in despair to my parents that I would never be able to save enough money for college. My parents tried to console[2] me, but it seemed impossible to save $64,268, the cost for the private institution that I desperately[3] wanted to attend.

Now let me tell you the amazing story of how I earned this sum of money.

It all began with a paper route in Ankeny, IA. I hated delivering that route, but was determined to stick it out for six months until my family moved to Wausau, WI. With a few meager[4] dollars from my paper route, a small nest egg began to develop. My next job was with an athletic company as a telephone customer service representative[5]. The savings account continued to grow very slowly. Then, the fall of my junior year of high school, I began to waitress at Denny's restaurant. It was hard work, but the money began to roll in and this job paid at least twice as much money per hour.

By the time my senior year arrived, I had saved a considerable[6] amount of money. This was encouraging, but I knew that I would also need some help, so began the process of applying for scholarships. Sometimes it was discouraging because I was rejected again and again. Then, my first scholarship offer came in, $2,000 a year to play tennis. This is only a small dent at a school that costs approximately[7] $14,000 a year, but it was a start. Sev-

我永远不会忘记我读高一时，有一天，我坐在通往地下室的楼梯上，双手抱着头，绝望地对父母哭诉说，我攒不够上大学的钱。我父母极力安慰我，但是要挣够 64,268 美元（这是我迫切想上的那所私立大学的费用），看来是不可能的。

现在让我告诉你我是如何挣够这笔钱的令人惊异的过程。

这一切开始于我在艾奥瓦州安克尼市送报纸的路上。我很讨厌那条送报路线，但我决心坚持干6个月，直到我家迁往威斯康星州的沃索市。拿着每次送报纸换来的几块钱，我的存款开始慢慢多起来。我的第二份工作是给一家运动员公司做电话客户服务代理。存折上的钱增长速度仍然很慢。之后，在上高二的秋季，我开始在丹尼斯餐馆当侍者。工作很辛苦，但钱来得快，每小时的报酬至少多出一倍。

等上了高三的时候，我已经存下了相当数目的钱。这真鼓舞人，但我知道我仍需要一些帮助，于是开始申请奖学金。有时很气馁，因为申请接二连三地遭到拒绝。后来我得到了第一笔奖学金，每年 2,000 美元，条件是为学校打网球。对于进这所大学每年大约要花费 14,000 美元来说，这

❶ descend /dɪˈsent/ *v.* 下来，下去，下降

❷ console /kənˈsəʊl/ *vt.* 安慰，慰问

❸ desperately /ˈdespərətlɪ/ *adv.* 拼命地，感到绝望而不惜冒险地

❹ meager /ˈmiːɡə/ *adj.* 少量的，不足的

❺ representative /ˌreprɪˈzentətɪv/ *n.* （公司的）代理，（尤指）派出的推销员

❻ considerable /kənˈsɪdərəbl/ *adj.* 相当多的，相当大的

❼ approximately /əˈprɒksɪmətlɪ/ *adv.* 大约，近乎正确或精确地

eral other academic scholarships also came my way and soon I was up to have $9,050 in scholarships. Between scholarships and savings, I had enough money for my first year!

Another interesting development emerged[8]. I began testing out of classes. Running anxiously to the mailbox in anticipation[9] of my test scores became part of my daily routine. Excitement mounted as test after test came back with passing results. Each passing result saved me to graduate a year early. This would save room and board expenses as well.

Finally, I was off to college. Because of careful saving, I did not have to work during the school year. Then, summer hit and it was time to work harder than ever. I continued working as a waitress at night, instructed tennis camps several mornings a week and worked as a secretary for a few hours in the afternoons. Being a little overzealous, I decided to also take a class at a community college. This class at the community college saved me $650. It was an exhausting summer and made me anxious[10] to return to my relatively easy life at college.

During my second and third years of undergraduate schooling, I decided to work about five hours per week in the campus admissions office answering phones. This provided a little spending money and kept me from draining my savings. The overall situation looked hopeful as I approached my senior year as long as I could make as much money as I had the previous[11] summer. That is when I decided to go to Israel to study for 3 weeks. I hesitated

只是杯水车薪，但仍不失为一个良好的开端。以后我又获得了几项学科奖学金，很快，奖学金的总额达到了9,050美元。有了奖学金和我自己的存款，第一年的学费足够了。

随后又有了趣味性的进展。我开始参加不同科目的免修考试。每天焦虑不安地冲向邮箱，盼望能拿到考试成绩，这成了我生活的一部分。当一个又一个考试通过的通知寄来时，我激动的心情也与之俱增。每通过一门科目的考试可节省约1,000美元的学费，并可让我提前一年毕业。这样还可以省下伙食费和住宿费。

大学的第二年和第三年，我决定每周在学校招生办公室工作5小时，工作是接听电话。这样我可以挣点零花钱，而不必动用积蓄。等快要进入第4年时，我对自己很有信心。只要暑假能再挣到上一个暑假那么多的钱就够了。可同时我还想去以色列学习3个星期。我犹豫不决，正要决定放弃，因为去以色列修学分要花费1,600多美元。大约两个星期以后，我妈妈打电话告诉我，我在银行里还存有1,600美元，而我早把它忘了！关于以色列之行，除了费用之外，另一个顾虑是失去了挣钱的时间。然而，那个暑假我

❽ **emerge**
/ɪˈmɜːdʒ/
vi. 显现，显露

❾ **anticipation**
/ænˌtɪsɪˈpeɪʃn/
n. 预料，预期，预测

❿ **anxious**
/ˈæŋkʃəs/
adj. 渴望的，担忧的

⓫ **previous**
/ˈpriːvɪəs/
adj. （事件或顺序上）在先的，前的

in making this decision and had just decided not to go because it would cost me $1,600 more to get the credits in Israel. About two weeks later my Mom called to tell me that I had $1,600 in the bank that I had forgotten about! One of my concerns about this trip was not only the cost, but the loss of time to make money; however, I made as much that summer in the ten weeks that I was home as I had made during the fourteen weeks that I was home the summer before. The way everything worked together to make this trip feasible was one of the most exciting things that has ever happened to me.

Finally, my senior year of college was upon me and to keep things interesting, I decided to buy a car. I obviously[12] did not have a lot of money to spend for a car and yet I wanted something reliable to make the ten-hour trips between home and school. I searched many newspaper ads and my father and I began searching for good used cars. I was ecstatic[13] when I found a crashed car that had been fixed up for only $4,200.

Then, I also attended an 8-week course on marriage and family in Colorado. This was an incredible[14] experience that taught me a great deal about my worldview and how to develop a healthy family. This experience was also very costly, $4,000. I was surprised to find that I had graduated with no debt and so many remarkable journeys along the way.

This experience has shaped me in many important ways. The first thing that I learned was the importance of a strong work eth-

在10个星期内挣下了相当于上个暑假14个星期挣的钱。各种巧合使得我的以色列之行得以实现，这是我一生所经历过的最激动人心的事情之一。

最后我进入大学的第四学年。为了能够事事称心，我决定买辆车。显然我没有过多的钱花在车上，但我需要一辆性能可靠的车，以便我能轻松地往返于家和学校之间（约10小时车程）。我搜寻了很多报纸上的广告，我爸爸和我一起查找性能良好的二手车信息。当我找到一辆撞毁后重新修复的车，只需4,200美元时，我欣喜若狂。

后来，我还参加了科罗拉多州的一个为期8周的关于婚姻和家庭的研习班。这是一次不可思议的经历，它改变了我的世界观，并教会了我如何建立一个健康的家庭。这次经历同时也花费了我4,000美元。等我毕业时我惊奇地发现，我没有任何负债，而且还在大学期间进行了那么多令人难忘的旅行。

这些经历在我身上产生了重大的影响。首先我学到了坚定的敬业精神的重要性。连续数小时长时间的工作塑造了我的性格，并让我懂得了每一元钱的价值。它还让我学会了在遇到难题时如何设计出有创意的解决办

⑫ **obviously** /ˈɒbvɪəslɪ/ *adv.* 明显，显然地

⑬ **ecstatic** /ɪkˈstætɪk/ *adj.* 欣喜若狂的，心醉神迷的

⑭ **incredible** /ɪnˈkredəbl/ *adj.* 难以置信的，不可思议的，惊人的

ic[15]. Working long hours did a lot to mold my character and helped me learn the value of a dollar. It also made me learn how to craft creative solutions to difficult dilemmas[16].

Whenever I am overwhelmed or afraid of the future, I can remember my $64,268 miracle.

法。

每当我对未来感到不知所措或惧怕时，我就会想到我那64,268美元的奇迹。

⑮ **ethic** /ˈeθɪk/

n. 道德标准，行为准则

⑯ **dilemma** /dɪˈlemə/

n. 进退两难的窘境，困难的选择

ABCs of courage

识字的勇气

I already went through life not being able to read to my own children. I want to be able to read to my granddaughter.

我这辈子已经经历了不能给自己的孩子读书的痛苦，我希望能够给我的孙女读书。

It is nearing dusk. The man is sitting in the dining room of Mrs. Patricia Lord, bending over a list of words.

The man is 55 years old. He is a large man, balding, and bears a resemblance to the actor Ernest Borgnine. He is in work clothes — denim[1] overalls, flannel[2] shirt. His hands are dirty from his labor. He drove here straight from a construction site where he works as a plumber[3].

The man never learned to read as a child. His mother was sick and his father was an alcoholic. The boy did not do well in school, and at the age of 12 he dropped out and began to work. Sometimes his mother would try to teach him something; his father, if he had been drinking, would say, "What the hell are you bothering to teach him for? He doesn't know anything."

The man went through most of his life hiding his secret. He learned to be a plumber; he married and started a family. He concealed his inability to read even from his wife and children; his wife did all the paper work around the house, read the mail, and handled the correspondence.

Then the man lost a job because he could not read. His company required each employee to take a written test about safety procedures. The man knew the rules, but could not read the questions.

Out of work, he felt panic. He enrolled in a nighttime course

天快黑了。这个男人正坐在帕特丽夏·罗德夫人的餐厅里，努力学习一张表上的单词。

这个男人55岁，他身材高大，秃头，而且长得有点像演员欧内斯特·本杰明。他穿着工作服——斜纹粗棉布❶的工作裤，法兰绒❷的衬衣。他的双手因劳动显得有些脏。他是从他做水暖工❸的那个建筑工地直接开车来这里的。

小时候这个男人从来没学过如何读书。他的妈妈有病，爸爸是个酒鬼。男孩儿在学校的成绩不好，12岁的时候他就辍学开始工作了。有时候他妈妈试着教他一些东西；他爸爸如果喝醉了酒，会说："你这么麻烦地教他是为了什么？他什么都知道。"

这个男人一生中的大部分时间都隐瞒着他的秘密。他学着成为一名水暖工人；结婚成立家庭，他甚至瞒着他的妻子和孩子他不认识字的这个事实；他妻子做家里所有和文字有关的工作，读信，回信。

然后这个男人因为不识字丢掉了工作。他的公司要求每位雇员参加一个关于安全程序的笔试。这个男人虽然知道这些条例，但他不会读题。

丢了工作，他感到恐慌。他报名参加了

❶ **denim** /ˈdenɪm/ *n.* 斜纹粗棉布

❷ **flannel** /ˈflænl/ *n.* 法兰绒

❸ **plumber** /ˈplʌmə/ *n.* 铅管工，水暖工

but soon realized that it was meant for people who at least knew the basics.

He bought a book called Reading Fun, designed for preschool-aged children. He looked at the pictures of ambulances[4] and taxis and trucks, followed by the word for each, and tried to teach himself. He couldn't.

Finally, he sat down with his wife. "You know when I lost my job? " he said. And he told her he couldn't read. He had wondered how she would react to his secret. "I'll help in any way I can," she said.

Several months later, from television, he heard about private tutoring offered by the Literacy Volunteers of Chicago. He called.

Patricia Lord, 59, remembered the first time he showed up at her door. "He was such a nice man. But it soon became clear — he didn't even know the alphabet[5]."

Twice a week they worked together. "He was so grateful," Mrs. Lord said. She taught him the alphabet. She taught him how to print letters. She taught him the first words other than his own name that he had never known how to read or write.

Since then, the man has found a new job. He keeps his reading cards in his truck and works on them during coffee breaks. His employers do not know that he cannot read; he is

一个夜校班，但很快发现这也是针对有一点儿基础的人的。

他买了一本书叫《乐趣阅读》，为学前儿童设计的。他努力自学，看着那些救护车、出租车、卡车的图片，紧跟着的是单词，但他仍不会。

最后，他和妻子坐在一起，“你知道我什么时候丢掉工作的吗？”他说。他告诉她他不识字。他想知道她对他的秘密有什么反应。“我会尽力帮助你，”她说。

几个月后，从电视上，他听说芝加哥的文化志愿者提供私人家教。于是他打了电话。

59岁的帕特丽夏·罗德记得他第一次出现在她门前时的样子。“他是一个非常好的人。但很快我就清楚了他甚至连字母表都不认识。”

他们一周一起学习两次。“他很好，”罗德夫人说。她教他字母表，教他如何写字母。她教他的第一个单词不是别的，而是他从来不知道如何认如何写的自己的名字。

然后，男人找到了一份新工作。他在他的卡车里带着认读卡片，在喝咖啡休息的时候学习。他的雇主不知道他不识字，他也很害怕他们会发现，他又会被解雇。

正是由于丢了另一份工作才使他决定不

❹ **ambulance** /ˈæmbjʊləns/ *n.* 救护车

❺ **alphabet** /ˈælfəbet/ *n.* 字母表

deathly afraid that they will find out and that he will be freed again.

It was losing the other job that convinced him he had to learn how to read. That and something else.

"I've got a little granddaughter," he said. "I never want her to come to me and say, 'Grandpa, read this,' and I can't do it. I already went through life not being able to read to my own children. I want to be able to read to my granddaughter.

He is proud of how far he has come in life. "I can take a blueprint and figure out how a whole building works," he said. "I built my own house. I think that's a pretty good accomplishment for a man who can't read.

"Still, I've had to pretend, all my life. In a restaurant, I'd pretend to read the menu[6]. But I didn't understand a word. I always asked the waitress what the specials were and choose one of them. I just did my best to keep it a secret.

"I've never written a letter in my life. When the holidays came, it was very hard for me to pick out a card for my wife. I'd looked at the cards, but I have no idea what they said. So I'd buy her a flower instead."

Now the dreams that before long he can really read something. "It doesn't have to be a lot. Mrs. Lord tells me that once

得不学习如何认字，还有其它事情。

“我有一个小孙女，”他说，“我再也不想她走过来对我说，‘爷爷，读读这个’，而我却不会。我这辈子已经经历了不能给自己的孩子读书的痛苦，我希望能够给我的孙女读书。”

他为一生中走过这么多而感到骄傲。“我可以勾勒出一幅蓝图，指出一整幢楼该如何施工，”他说，“我建造我自己的房子，我想这对于一个不认识字的人来说是个杰作。

“我还是不得不隐瞒了一辈子。在饭店，我假装看菜单。但是我一个字都不认识。我总是问服务员特色菜是什么，然后选一个。我尽力保守这个秘密。

“我这一辈子从没写过信。假日到来时，给妻子寄张贺卡对于我来说非常困难。我看过一些贺卡，但我不知道它们说些什么。所以我给她买了一束花。”

现在的梦想是不久之后他能认识一些东西。“不需要太多。罗德夫人告诉我，一旦你开始了，就会变得更容易。

“如果我这一天学得不好，并且忘记了很多词，我就会厌恶自己。但当我学得好时我就会兴高采烈。我会回家告诉妻子，‘我学

❻ **menu** /ˈmenjuː/ *n.* 菜单

you start, it comes easier all the time.

"I get disgusted with[7] myself if I have a bad day and miss a lot of words. But when there has been a good day I'll feel great. I'll go home and tell my wife, 'I learned this word.' Or I'll say, 'Teacher says I have good handwriting.' And then my wife and I will work on the spelling cards."

It is getting dark outside. The man has been up since before dawn. At the dining-room table, Mrs. Lord is helping him write a sentence.

"I can't wait until I can write a letter," he says. "The first is going to be to my wife. I'm going to tell her how much I love her."

了这个词。’或者我会说‘老师说我写字很漂亮。’然后我和妻子会一起学习拼写卡片。”

外边天渐渐黑了。男人天亮前就起来了。在餐厅的桌子旁，罗德夫人正在教他写一句话。

“我要等到我能写一封信，”他说，“首先我要写给我妻子，我要告诉她我是多么地爱她。”

❼ **get disgusted with**
对…感到厌恶

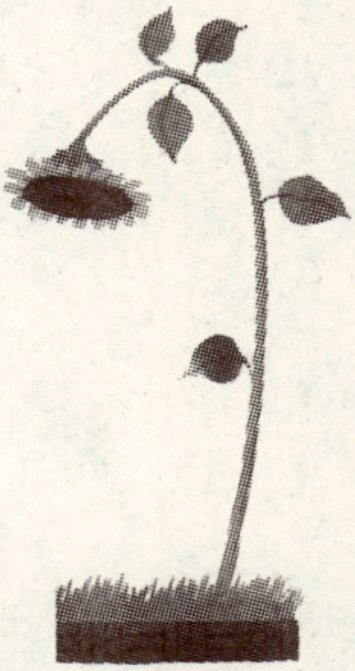

Say yes to yourself

对自己说是

By reorienting, you can learn to see yourself and the world around you differently.

通过重新调整方向，你可以学着从一个不同的角度看你自己和这个世界。

It's the classic story with a twist: a traveling salesman gets a flat tire on a dark, lonely road and then discovers he has no jack[1]. He sees a light in a farmhouse. As he walks toward it, his mind churns: "Suppose no one comes to the door." "Suppose they don't have a jack." "Suppose the guy won't lend me his jack even if he has one." The harder his mind works, the more agitated he becomes, and when the door opens, he punches[2] the farmer and said yells, "Keep your lousy[3] jack! "

That story brings a smile, because it pokes fun at[4] a common type of self-defeatist thinking. How often have you heard yourself say: "Nothing ever goes the way I planned." "I'll never make that deadline," "I always screw up."

Such inner speech shapes your life more than any other single force. Like it or not, you travel through life with your thoughts spell gloom and doom, that's where you're headed, because put-down[5] words sabotage[6] confidence instead of offering support and encouragement.

Simply put, to feel better, you need to think better. Here's how:

1. *Tune into your thoughts.* The first thing Sue said to her new therapist[7] was, " I know you can't help me, Doctor. I'm a total mess. I keep lousing up at work, and I'm sure I'm going to be canned. Just yesterday my boss told me I was being transferred. He called it promotion. But if I was doing a good job, why transfer

这是一个曲折的经典小故事：一个巡回推销员在一条漆黑偏僻的路上，一条车胎瘪了，但是发现又没有千斤顶。他看见一家农舍亮着灯，一边往那走，他脑子里一边翻江倒海地想："假如没人开门。""假如他们没有千斤顶。""假如那个家伙有千斤顶却不借给我。"他越想越生气，当门打开时，他挥拳猛打了农民一下，喊道："留着你的破千斤顶吧！"

这个故事引人发笑，因为它嘲弄了一种普遍的自我挫败者的想法。你会常常对自己说这样的话吗："没有一件事和我计划的一样，""我在最后期限内永远不可能完成，""我总是把事情弄糟。"

正是这些来自内心的话语而不是其他 的任何力量造就了你的生活。不管你是否喜欢，你的一生会在犹豫和绝望中度过，这成了你前进的方向，因为羞辱的言语不会给予支持和鼓励，只会破坏信心。

简单地说，要想感觉更好，你必须想得更好。这里有一些方法：

1.*与你的想法保持一致*。苏对她的新的治疗专家说的第一件事是："我知道你帮不了我，医生。我是个一点都不整洁的人。我总是把工作搞糟，而且我确信我很快就会被

❶ **jack** /dʒæk/ *n.* 千斤顶

❷ **punch** /pʌntʃ/ *v.* 用拳猛击

❸ **lousy** /ˈlaʊzɪ/ *adj.* 极坏的

❹ **poke fun at** 嘲弄或嘲笑

❺ **put-down** 羞辱的

❻ **sabotage** /ˈsæbətɑːʒ/ *v.* 破坏

❼ **therapist** /ˈθerəpɪst/ *n.* 治疗专家

me? ”

Then, gradually, Sue's story moved past the put-downs. She had received her M.B.A. two years before and was making an excellent salary. That didn't sound like failure.

At the end of their first meeting, Sue's therapist told her to jot[8] down her thoughts, particularly at night if she was having trouble falling asleep. At her next appointment Sue's list included: "I'm not really smart. I got ahead by a bunch of flukes[9]." "Tomorrow will be a disaster. I've never chaired a meeting before." "My boss looked furious this morning. What did I do? "

She admitted, "In one day alone, I listed 26 negative thoughts. No wonder I'm always tired and depressed."

Hearing her fears and forebodings[10] read out loud made Sue realize how much energy she was squandering[11] on imagined catastrophes. If you've been feeling down, it could be you're sending yourself negative message too. Listen to the words churning inside your head. Repeat them aloud or write them down, if that will help capture them.

With practice, turning in will become automatic. As you are walking or driving down the street, you can hear your silent broadcast. Soon your thoughts will do your bidding, rather than the other way round. And when that happens, your feelings and actions will change too.

封闭起来。昨天我的老板告诉我，我被换工作了。他把这叫做升职，但是如果我工作得很好，为什么调动我？”

然后，渐渐地，苏的故事里不都是这些泄气的话了。两年前她就拿下了MBA，而且薪水不菲，这听起来不像失败。

在他们第一次见面快要结束的时候，苏的医生告诉她记下她的想法，尤其是在晚上睡不着觉的时候。下次见面时苏带来的记录包括这样的话：“我真的不聪明，我由于侥幸才超过了别人。”“明天会大难临头，我以前从来没主持过会议。”“今天早晨我的老板看起来好像生气了。我做错了什么？”

她承认：“仅仅一天，我列出了26条消极的想法。难怪我总是很累很消沉。”

把她的恐惧和不祥的预感大声读出来之后，苏意识到她在想象的灾难上浪费了多少精力。如果你感觉低落，可能也是因为你给了自己消极的信息。听一听你大脑中反复出现的话，大声重复出来或写下来，如果这样可以帮助你捕捉住它们的话。

通过练习，表现出色会变得十分自然。当你在街上走路或开车时，你不再胡思乱想了。很快，你的想法为你服务，而不再是你听从于你的想法。如果做到这些，你的感觉

❽ **jot** /dʒɒt/
v. 匆匆记下

❾ **fluke** /fluːk/
n. 侥幸的成功

❿ **foreboding** /fɔːˈbəʊdɪŋ/
n. 不详的预感

⓫ **squander** /ˈskwɒndə/
v. 浪费

2. *Isolate destructive words and phrases.* Fran's inner voice kept telling her she was "only a secretary." Mark's reminded him he was "just a salesman." With the word only or just, they were downgrading their jobs and, by extension, themselves.

By isolating negative words and phrases, you can pinpoint the damage you're doing to yourself. For Fran and Mark, the culprits[12] were only and just. Once those words are eliminated, there's nothing destructive about saying "I am a salesman" or "I am a secretary." Both statements open doors to positive follow-ups, such as, "I'm on my way up the ladder."

3. *Stop the thought.* Short-circuit negative messages as soon as they start by using the one-word command stop!

In theory, stopping is a simple technique. In practice, it's not as easy as it sounds. To be effective at stopping, you have to be forceful and tenacious[13]. Raise your voice when you give the command. Picture yourself drowning out the inner voice of fear.

4. *Accentuate the positive.* There's a story about a man who went to a psychiatrist. "What's the trouble?" asked the doctor.

"Two months ago my grandfather died and left me $75,000. Last month, a cousin passed away and left me $100,000."

"Then why are you depressed?"

和行动也会改变。

2. *隔离具有破坏性的句子和词语。*弗兰来自内心的声音总是告诉她：她“只是一个秘书”，马克被提醒：他“只不过是一个推销员”。通过“只”或“只不过”这些词，他们贬低了他们的工作甚至他们自己。

通过隔绝消极的句子和词语，你可以准确指出你正在伤害自己。对于弗兰和马克来说，是“只”和“只不过”这两个词的错。一旦删掉这些词，说“我是个推销员”或“我是个秘书”没有任何坏处。这两句话都可能向积极的方向发展，比如，“我正在逐步升职的过程中。”

3. *停止消极的想法。*只要一有消极的想法就通过“停”这个只有一个字的命令使之停止！

从理论上来说，停是一个简单的技巧，实际上，它却没有听起来那么简单。要想有效地停止，你必须有力并且坚决。当你下命令时要提高嗓音，想象它压过了你内心恐惧的声音。

4. *强调积极。*这个故事讲的是一个人到精神专家那里。“怎么了？”医生问。

“两个月前我爷爷去世了，给我留下了75,000 美元；上个月我堂兄去世留给我

⑫ **culprit**
/ˈkʌlprɪt/
n. 犯罪者

⑬ **tenacious**
/tɪˈneɪʃəs/
adj. 坚决的

⑭ **exorcise**
/ˈeksɔːsaɪz/
v. 消除

"This month, *nothing*!"

When a person is in a depressed mood, everything can seem depressing. So once you've exorcised[14] the demons by calling a stop, replace them with good thoughts.

One person described the process this way: "Every night I used to lie awake with a whirlpool of thoughts spinning in my head: 'Was I too harsh with the children?' 'Did I forget to return that client's call?'"

"Finally, when I was at my wits' end[15], I thought about the wonderful day with Jenny at the zoo. I recalled how she laughed at the chimps. Soon my head was filled with pleasant emotions, and I fell asleep."

5. *Reorient[16] yourself.* Have you ever been feeling down late in the day, when someone suddenly said, "Let's go out"? Remember how your spirits picked up? You changed the direction of your thinking, and your mood brightened.

Reorient yourself right now. You are tense because you must finish a huge project by Friday. On Saturday you plan to go shopping with friends. Reorient from "Friday workload" to "Saturday fun."

By reorienting, you can learn to see yourself and the world around you differently. If you think you can do something, you in-

100,000美元。”

“那你为什么忧愁呢?”

“这个月，什么都没有!”

当一个人消沉时，每件事都令人沮丧。所以一旦你通过喊停消除了恶魔，就用积极的想法代替它们吧。

一个人这样形容这个过程：“每天晚上我都躺着睡不着，一堆想法在我脑子里转：‘我是不是对孩子太严厉了?’‘我是不是忘记回客户的电话了?’”

“最后，当我没的可想时，我想和珍妮在动物园渡过的美好的一天，又想起她怎么笑话那些大猩猩，很快我脑子里充满了愉快的情感，我就睡着了。”

5. *重新调整方向*。快天黑的时候你是否曾经感觉不好，当有人突然说：“让我们出去怎么样?”，你的精神又好起来了，是不是?改变你思考的方向，你的心情就会变好。

现在重新调整好你自己。你紧张是因为周五前你必须完成一项大工程，周六你打算和朋友一起去购物。从“周五的工作负担”转到“周六的愉快”上。

通过重新调整方向，你可以学着从一个不同的角度看你自己和这个世界。如果你认为你可以做什么事，你成功的几率就大。乐

⑮ **at one's wits's end**
智穷计尽；不知所措

⑯ **reorient**
/riːˈɔːrɪənt/
v. 重新设定方向

crease your chances of doing it. Optimism gets you moving. Depressing thoughts bog you down[17], because you are thinking, "What's the use?"

Make it a habit to remember your best self, the you that you want to be. In particular, remember things for which you have been complimented. That's the real you. Make this the frame of reference for your life — a picture of you at your best.

观使你前进，消沉使你停滞，因为你正在想“有什么用”？

要养成这个习惯：记住最优秀的自己，你理想中的自己。尤其是，记住那些你曾被别人称赞的事情。这是真实的你，把这作为你人生的参照，一张你处于最佳状态的图片。

⑰ **bog sth down**

(使)陷入泥沼

Take charge of your life

掌控你的生命

Paul isn't sure why he got that flash of insight. But the moment changed his life and freed him "to be myself in what had become my world."

保罗不确定他为什么恍然大悟。但那一刻改变了他的一生，并且把他从“我自己的世界中的自己”解放出来。

Julio Iglesias was a professional soccer player in Madrid when a car crash ended his career and left him paralyzed for a year and a half. A sympathetic[1] nurse gave Iglesias a guitar to help pass the time in the hospital. Though had no prior musical aspirations[2], Iglesias went on to become a huge success in the pop-music field.

Iglesias's accident marked a watershed[3] in his life, a turning point after which everything changed. A watershed can come in the form of an illness, an accident or a random encounter; it can be any event, positive or negative, that significantly affects the course of a person's life. After interviewing 632 people, we've come up with four strategies for mastering life's unpredictable moments and transforming them into opportunities for growth:

Assume responsibility for yourself

Amy was divorced by her husband after 24 years of marriage. With neither the education to pursue a particular career nor the belief in herself to support such a move, she could have slipped into self-pity and stagnated[4].

Instead, she took responsibility for herself. "I wanted to move beyond the hurt and make something of my life," she says. "So I took a real-estate course, got my license and eventually opened my own office. Soon I'll be one of the largest independent brokers[5] in this city."

Julio Iglesias 是马德里的一名职业足球运动员，但是一场车祸结束了他的职业生涯，并且使他瘫痪了一年半。一位好心的护士给了他一把吉他，帮他渡过在医院的日子。尽管他以前没有音乐方面的志向，他坚持练习并在流行音乐界取得了巨大的成功。

Iglesias 的事故成了他生命中的转折点，在这之后所有的事情都改变了。转折点可能以疾病、故事或偶遇的形式出现，它可能是积极的也可能是消极的事情，它在很大程度上影响了一个人一生的历程。在采访了 632 个人之后，我总结了四条掌控生命中不可预见的时刻，并把它们变为成长机会的策略：

对自己负责

结婚 24 年后艾米的丈夫和她离婚了。既没有知识可以找到一份特别的工作，也不相信自己可以支撑如此大的变故，她可能会陷入自怜自悯和停滞不前之中。

她没有这样，而是对自己负起了责任。“我想战胜伤害，做出人生的一番事业，”她说。“所以我参加了学习不动产的课程，得到了经营许可证并最终开了一个属于我自己的办公室。很快我成了这个城市里最大的独立经纪人之一。”

❶ **sympathetic** /ˌsɪmpəˈθetɪk/ *adj.* 表示同情的，讨人喜欢的

❷ **aspiration** /ˌæspəˈreɪʃn/ *n.* 渴望，抱负，志气

❸ **watershed** /ˈwɔːtəʃed/ *n.* 分水岭，事情发展中的转折点

❹ **stagnate** /stægˈneɪt/ *v.* 停滞，变迟钝

❺ **broker** /ˈbrəʊkə/ *n.* 经纪人

Make tough choices

The range of experiences people defined as watersheds was considerable. Women were far more likely to cite problems with other people. Men typically mentioned experiences related to education or career. Those who gained most through such experiences felt it is not possible to grow because of the decisions they make.

David Hartman, the former host of ABC-TV's "Good Morning America," graduates from college with a degree in economics. Many attractive business opportunities beckoned[6], but Hartman — who had worked part-time in college as a radio and TV announcer — made a tough decision. He turned his back on[7] years of academic training and, forgoing[8] financial security, began a career in the highly uncertain entertainment/communications field.

Risk frequently pays large dividends[9]. The career of entertainer[10] Mary Martin took off after a talent show at a Hollywood nightclub. She sang a waltz called "Il Bacio." For fun, she decided to jazz up the middle part. She began in traditional fashion, in her best operatic voice. Then she let loose. She finished to a standing ovation[11] and a new career.

Seek relationships that enrich your life

Even a casual acquaintance or a stranger may have a deep impact on our lives. Near the height of his career, baseball great Roy Campanella was paralyzed in an accident. About a year later, he was sitting in his wheelchair at a ballpark[12] when an elderly

做艰苦的决定

大卫·哈特曼，前ABC电视台“美国您早”节目的主持人，上大学时是学经济的，许多极具吸引力的公司提供的机会吸引着他，但是哈特曼（大学期间曾做过电台和电视台的兼职播音员）做了一个艰苦的决定。他避开了有着多年学术训练的领域，放弃了财政保障，开始了在毫无保障的娱乐/传播领域的生涯。

冒险经常很有好处。表演家马瑞·马丁的职业生涯是从好莱坞夜总会一次天才的演出开始的。她唱了一曲华尔兹叫“Il Bacio”。为了好玩，她决定用爵士乐风格演唱中间部分。她用自己最好的适于歌剧的嗓音以传统的方式开始，然后她的声音放松下来。结束后人们都站了起来为她鼓掌，她也开始了一段新的生涯。

寻找丰富生活的关系

甚至一个偶然的路人或一个陌生人可能都对我们的一生有重大的影响。在快要达到事业巅峰时，著名的棒球运动员罗伊·坎帕内拉在一场意外事故中瘫痪了。大约一年后，在棒球场，他在轮椅上坐着，这时一位老妇人向他走来。她腿上夹着夹具，用拐杖走路。

当这个陌生人走到他面前时，她握住了罗伊无助的双手感谢他给了她生活下去的勇气。她也曾住在他以前住的那家纽约医院里。在她

⑥ **beckon**
/ˈbekən/
v. 召唤，吸引

⑦ **turn one's back on**
避开或拒绝接受

⑧ **forgo**
/fɔːˈɡəʊ/
v. 放弃或没有也行

⑨ **pay dividends**
产生效益，得到好处

⑩ **entertainer**
/ˌentəˈteɪnə/
n. 表演者，艺人

⑪ **ovation**
/əʊˈveɪʃn/
n. 热烈鼓掌或欢呼

⑫ **ballpark**
/ˈbɔːlˈpɑːk/
n. 棒球场

woman worked her way up to him. She had braces on her legs, and walked with a crutch.

When the stranger reached Campanella, she took his helpless hand in hers and thanked him for giving her the courage to live. She had been a patient in the same New York hospital he had been in. After a stroke paralyzed one side of her body, she gave up on life. But doctors at the hospiotal told her about Campanella's courage, and the woman was so inspired by his story that she determined to make the effort to live. She later traveled over a thousand miles to thank him in person, thus giving back to Campanella some of the inspiration and courage that he had instilled in her.

Affirm self-worth

Take Paul, for instance, a successful newspaper reporter in a large city. He came to this country, at the age of six, as a refugee. His early experiences as a schoolboy who could speak no English were painful. He found himself either fighting over or running from the taunts[13] of his classmates, and developed what he calls a "refugee mentality." This showed up in such typical sentiments as "Don't make waves," "Be thankful you're here," "It's not your turn."

Then came a summer-camp job in 1967 — and with it a turning point. "The most prestigious[14] position at the camp, that of waterfront[15] director, was offered to me because I had the necessary qualifications," Paul told us. "As usual, I heard this voice in my

半边身体瘫痪后，她真的不想活了。但医院的医生给她讲罗伊是多么的勇敢，他的故事鼓舞了她，她决定努力活下去。事后，她跑了大约一千里的路来亲自感谢罗伊，把他给她的鼓舞和勇气再返还给他一些。

肯定自我价值

保罗是一个大都市成功的新闻记者，6 岁时流亡到这个国家，小时候上学时他不会说英语，这种经历很痛苦。他发现自己或者和同学争吵或者从他们的嘲笑中逃跑，形成了一种“难民思想”，并在这样一些典型的思想中表现出来，如：“不要惹事生非”，“你在这里就知足吧”，“这还轮不到你”。

后来，1967 年的夏令营工作成了一个转折点。“我成了夏令营中滨水区的指挥，因为我有必要的资历，这个工作很有影响力。”保罗对我们说：“像通常一样，我听到大脑中有这样一个声音在提醒我：（这还轮不到你赢，你不是什么重要人物）。出乎意料的是，我得到了这个职位，好像一盏灯被打开了。‘某一天’就是现在。轮到我了，所以我说是。”

保罗不确定他为什么恍然大悟。但那一刻改变了他的一生，并且把他从“我自己的

⑬ **taunt** /tɔːnt/
n. 嘲笑，讥讽

⑭ **prestigious** /preˈstɪdʒəs/
adj. 有影响力的，有威信的

⑮ **waterfront** /ˈwɔːtəˈfrɒnt/
n. 滨水路，滨水区

head reminding me, It's not your turn to win. You're not on the first string. Unexpectedly, like a light being switched on[16], it all fell into place. 'Someday' was now. It was my turn. So I said yes."

Paul isn't sure why he got that flash of insight. But the moment changed his life and freed him "to be myself in what had become my world."

世界中的自己”解放出来。

⑯ **switch on**

接通;开

A conversation between success and failure

成功与失败的对话

There are three things that a person must know to survive long in the world: what is too much, what is too little, and what is just right for him or her.

一个人必须知道三件事才能在这个世界上活得时间更长：什么是太多，什么是太少，什么是正好。

Life for us has become an endless succession of contests. From the moment the alarm clock rings until sleep overtakes us again, from the time we are toddlers[1] until the day we die, we are busy struggling to outdo others. This is our posture at work and at school, on the playing field and back at home. It is the common denominator of American life.

I know a little about competition, about winning and losing, about success and failure. At the age of eight or nine, my sister and I would play Monopoly from time to time. If she happened to buy the two most expensive properties, Boardwalk and Park Place, and then begin to build them up, I knew how things would inevitably end. I would land on one of the two and lose all of my money. Better, I thought, at such a time to avoid failure by simply picking the game board up and flinging it into the air to bring the game to a premature[2] end. I didn't lose or concede[3] defeat, I simply stopped playing. Long before the age of eight I knew what losing was, and I didn't like it. This is called being averse[4] to failure.

In a competitive environment failure is a foe and success is a friend. Or as Vince Lombardi once said, "Winning isn't everything; it's the only thing." Perhaps if professional football were all of life, Lombardi's conclusion would be part of the spiritual wisdom of the ages, but it isn't. While he was a good football coach, he was not a sage[5].

A similar sentiment was expressed in the Jason Miller's play,

生活对于我们来说已经变成了一个接一个没有尽头的竞赛。从闹钟响起到上床睡觉，从我们刚学会走路一直到去世，我们忙着努力超过别人。这是我们在单位、在学校、在球场和在家的态度。这也是美国生活的共同特点。

我对竞赛、输赢、成功和失败了解不多。我8、9岁时，偶尔和姐姐玩大富豪游戏。如果她碰巧买了两个最贵的道具、木板路、停车场，然后使它们增值，我知道事情将会是如何不可避免的结束。我会站在其中一个上面，并且输掉我所有的钱。我认为在那样的时刻避免失败更好的方法是，拿起游戏板扔到空中使这个游戏提前结束。我没有输或承认失败，我只是不玩了。很久以前，我8岁时知道了失败是什么，并且不喜欢它。这被称作讨厌失败。

在竞争的环境中，失败是敌人，成功是朋友。或者像文斯·隆巴蒂曾经说过的那样："胜利不是全部，它只是一件事。"也许如果职业足球是生命的全部，隆巴蒂的结论会成为成年人精神智慧的一部分，但它不是。当他是一个优秀的足球教练时，他不是圣人。

在詹森·米勒的戏剧《冠军赛季》中也表述了相似的看法。教练告诉一名队员："奖杯是真理，惟一的真理。"我不反对比赛，但

❶ **toddler**
/ˈtɒdlə/
n. 刚学会走路的孩子

❷ **premature**
/ˈprematjuə/
adj. 提前的，过早的

❸ **concede**
/kənˈsiːd/
v. 承认某事属实

❹ **averse**
/əˈvɜːs/
adj. 不喜欢或反对某事

❺ **sage** /seɪdʒ/
n. 圣人，贤哲

"The Championship Season." The coach tells a player, "The trophy is the truth, the only truth." I am not opposed to competition, but we need to teach our children about the limits of competition, otherwise the source of their self-esteem and the way they judge themselves will become increasingly influenced by external circumstances.

Better, I think, to acquaint them with the wisdom of people like Henry David Thoreau who wrote, Why should we be in such desperate haste to succeed, and in such desperate enterprises? If a man [or a woman] does not keep pace with their companions, perhaps it is because they hear a different drummer.

At the level of popular culture we worship success and condemn failure. It is ironic that many people see success as completely of their own making and failure as largely influenced by events beyond their control. These formulas are reversed when it is applied to others. Success is the work of fate and failure is solely the responsibility and fault of the individual.

John Holt wrote that many people desire to win so that they might have "the ignoble[6] satisfaction of feeling that they are better than someone else." And yet that is never the path to true maturity. To quote Carlos Castaneda, "such a path has no heart."

Popular culture would have us believe that success and failure are entirely dissimilar, opposed outcomes. And yet I am more intrigued[7] with their similarities. I believe that they are two sides of

我们需要教给我们的孩子竞赛的短处，否则他们自尊的源泉和评价自己的方法将越来越多地受外部环境影响。

我认为最好让他们熟悉像亨利·大卫·梭罗这样的智者，他写过这样的话：我们为什么拼命地急着要成功，并且是从事成功的希望非常渺茫的事业。如果一个男人（或女人）未能和他们的同伴保持同步的话，也许因为他们听到了不同节奏的声音。

在流行文化这一层面我们崇敬成功，谴责失败。具有讽刺意味的是，许多人把成功完全看作自己的功劳，失败主要受超出他们控制的事情的影响。这些模式应用到他人身上正好相反，成功是命中注定，失败全是他们个人的责任和错误。

约翰·霍特写道：许多人想成功，所以他们也许有“感到自己比别人优秀的这种不光彩的满足感”。但这永远不会成为走向真正成熟的道路。引用卡洛斯·卡斯坦达的一句话：“这样的路没有核心。”

流行文化使我们相信成功和失败是完全不同的，是相反的结果。但是我对它们的相同点更感兴趣。我相信它们是同一枚硬币的两面。它们都能教给我们生活和智慧。一个马拉维的谚语说：“一个人必须知道三件事

❻ **ignoble** /ɪɡˈnəʊbl/ *adj.* 不光彩的，卑鄙的，可耻的

❼ **intrigue** /ɪnˈtriːɡ/ *v.* 激起某人的兴趣或好奇心

the same coin. Both have the ability to teach us about life and about wisdom. A Malawi proverb[8] states that, "There are three things that a person must know to survive long in the world: what is too much, what is too little, and what is just right for him or her." Our experience of success and failure helps to teach us these lessons that we might live our lives fully and well.

才能在这个世界上活得时间更长：什么是太多，什么是太少，什么是正好。”我们成功和失败的经验教会我们这些重要的知识，使我们的生活美满幸福。

❽ **proverb**
/ˈprɒvɜːb/
n. 谚语

A seven-dollar dream

一个七美元的梦想

My violin began to sing again those favorite tunes that had never left my memory.

我的小提琴开始再次发出那些我喜欢的而且从未离我记忆而去的旋律。

Wanted: Violin. Can't pay much. Call...

Why did I notice that? I wondered, since I rarely look at the classified ads. I laid the paper on my lap and closed my eyes, remembering what had during the Great Depression, when my family struggled[1] to make a living on our farm. I, too, had wanted a violin, but we didn't have the money...

When my older twin sisters began showing an interest in music, Harriet Anne learned to play Grandma's upright piano, while Suzanne turned to Daddy's violin. Simple tunes soon became lovely melodies[2] as the twins played more and more. Caught up in the rhythm[3] of the music, my baby brother danced around while Daddy hummed and Mother whistled. I just listened.

When my arms grew long enough, I tried to play Suzanne's violin, I loved the mellow[4] sound of the firm bow drawn across the strings. Oh, how I wanted one! But I knew it was out of the question.

One evening as the twins played in the school orchestra[5], I closed my eyes tight to capture the picture firmly in my mind. Someday, I'll sit up there, I vowed silently.

It was not a good year. At harvest the crops did not bring as much as we had hoped, I couldn't wait any longer to ask, "Daddy, may I have a violin of my own?"

求购：小提琴。付不起太多钱。请打电话给……

我为什么注意那个呢？我感到奇怪，因为我很少看分类广告。

我把报纸放在大腿上，闭上眼睛，想起了很多年前发生的事情。在大萧条时期，那时我的父亲努力工作维持我们在农场的生活。我也曾想要一个小提琴，但是我们没有钱……

当我的双胞胎姐姐表现出对音乐的兴趣，哈里特·安学着弹外婆的竖式钢琴，苏珊娜也开始学拉爸爸的小提琴。随着双胞胎练习得越来越多，简单的曲调很快变成了优美的旋律。沉浸在音乐的节奏中，我弟弟跳起了舞，同时爸爸也哼着曲子，妈妈用口哨吹着调子，我只是听着。

当我的胳膊长到足够长，我试着拉苏珊娜的小提琴。我喜欢坚实的琴弓在弦上拉过时柔和的声音。噢，我多么想要一只小提琴呀！但是我知道那是不可能的。

一天傍晚，当双胞胎姐妹在学校管弦乐队演奏时，我紧闭双眼尽力把这些景象牢记于脑海中。我默默地发誓，总有一天我也要坐在那里。

这不是一个好的年景。收获的时候庄稼

❶ **struggle**
/ˈstrʌgl/
v. 努力，奋斗，挣扎

❷ **melody**
/ˈmelədɪ/
n. 主调，旋律，主旋律

❸ **rhythm**
/ˈrɪðəm/
n. 节奏

❹ **mellow**
/ˈmeləʊ/
adj. （颜色或声音）柔和的，丰富的

❺ **orchestra**
/ˈɔːkɪstrə/
n. 管弦乐队

"Can't you use Suzanne's?"

"I'd like to be in the orchestra, too, and we can't both use the same violin at the same time."

Daddy's face looked sad. That night, and many following nights, I heard him remind God in our family devotions[6], "...and Lord, Mary Lou wants her own violin."

One evening we all sat around the table. The twins and I studied. Mother sewed, and Daddy wrote a letter to his friend, George Finkle, in Columbus. Mr. Finkle, Daddy said, was a fine violinist.

As he wrote, Daddy read parts of his letter out loud to Mother. Weeks later I discovered he'd written one line he didn't read aloud: "Would you watch for a violin for my third daughter? I can't pay much, but she enjoys music, and we'd like her to have her own instrument."

When Daddy received a letter from Columbus a few weeks later, he announced, "We'll be driving to Columbus to spend the night with Aunt Alice as soon as I can find someone to care for the livestock[7]."

At last the day arrived, and we drove to Aunt Alice's. After we arrived, I listened while Daddy made a phone call. He hung up and asked, "Mary Lou, do you want to go with me to visit Mr.

没有我们希望的产量高。尽管日子很艰苦，我还是迫不及待地要求，“爸爸，我可以有一个属于我自己的小提琴吗?”

“你难道不能用苏珊娜的吗?”

“我也想参加管弦乐队，我们俩不能同时用同一把小提琴。”

爸爸的脸色看上去很悲伤。那个晚上以及接下来的许多个晚上，我听到父亲在全家祈祷时提醒上帝，“……并且耶稣·基督，玛丽·卢想要一把属于她自己的小提琴。”

一天傍晚，我们都围坐在桌边，我和双胞胎姐妹在学习。妈妈正在缝衣服，爸爸给他在哥伦布的朋友乔治·菲克写信。爸爸说菲克先生是一位杰出的小提琴家。

当爸爸写信时，他把其中的部分内容大声地读给妈妈听。几周以后我发现，爸爸有一行内容没有大声读出来：“您能帮助我的三女儿找一把小提琴吗？我付不起太多的钱，但是她喜欢音乐，并且我也希望她有属于自己的乐器。”

几周后，当爸爸收到一封从哥伦布的来信时，他宣布，“我一旦找到人看管我们的牲畜，我们就开车去哥伦布和艾丽丝姨妈那里。”

终于等到了这一天，我们开车去了艾丽

❻ **devotion**
/dɪˈvəʊʃn/
n. 祈祷，宗教仪式

❼ **livestock**
/ˈlaɪvstɒk/
n. 家畜，牲畜（如牛羊）

Finkle? ”

“Sure,” I answered.

He drove into a residential area and stopped in the driveway[8] of a fine, old house. We walked up the steps and rang the door chime. A tall man, older than Daddy, opened the door. “Come in! ” He and Daddy heartily[9] shook hands, both talking at once.

“Mary Lou, I’ve been hearing things about you. Your daddy has arranged a big surprise for you! ” Mr. Finkle ushered us into the parlor[10]. He picked up a case, opened it, lifted out a violin and started to play. The melody surged[11] and spoke like waterfalls. Oh, to play like him, I thought.

Finishing the number[12], he turned to Daddy. “Carl, I found it in a pawnshop[13] for seven dollars. It’s a good violin. Mary Lou should be able to make beautiful music with it.” Then he handed the violin to me.

I noticed the tears in Daddy’s eyes as I finally comprehended. It was mine! I stroked the violin gently. The wood was a golden brown that seemed to warm in the light. “It’s beautiful,” I said, barely breathing.

When we arrived back at Aunt Alice’s, all eyes turned as we entered. I saw Daddy wink at Mother, and then I realized everyone had known but me. I know Daddy’s prayer, and mine, had

丝姨妈家。到了之后，我听见爸爸打了一个电话，他挂断之后问：“玛丽·卢，你希望和我一起去拜访菲克先生吗?”

“当然想。”我回答。

他开车到了一个住宅区，停在了一所漂亮的老房子的车道上。我们走上台阶并按了门铃。一个高大的，比父亲的年龄大一些男人开了门说：“请进！”他和爸爸热情地握手，两个人都立刻说起话来。

“玛丽·卢，我听说过你的事情。你爸爸为你安排了一个大惊喜！”菲克先生把我们带到了客厅，他拿起一个盒子，打开，取出一把小提琴开始演奏，旋律像瀑布一样波浪前进。噢，演奏得像他一样，我想。

拉完一曲后，他转向爸爸，“卡尔，我在一个当铺发现了它，花了7美元。这是一把很好的小提琴。玛丽·卢应该能用它演奏出动听的音乐。”然后菲克先生把琴给了我。

我看到爸爸眼中的泪水时我终于明白了，它是我的了！我轻轻地抚摸着琴，木头是金棕色的，在灯光下看起来很温暖。“它很漂亮。”我说，几乎屏住了呼吸。

当我们回到艾丽丝姨妈家时，我们一进来，所有的眼睛都转向了我们。我看到爸爸向妈妈眨眼，之后我意识到除了我大家都知

❽ **driveway**
/ˈdraɪvweɪ/
n. （通往住宅的）私人车道

❾ **heartily**
/ˈhɑːtɪlɪ/
adv. 尽情地，热心地，痛快地

❿ **parlor**
/ˈpɑːlə/
n. 起居室，客厅，会客厅

⓫ **surge**
/sɜːdʒ/
v. 在波涛中或如同波浪般前进

⓬ **number**
/ˈnʌmbə/
n. 一首歌，一段舞蹈

⓭ **pawnshop**
/ˈpɔːnʃɒp/
n. 当铺

been answered.

The day I carried my violin to school for my first lesson no one could imagine the bursting feeling in my heart. Over the moths I practiced daily, feeling the warm wood fit under my chin like an extension of myself.

When I was ready to join the school orchestra, I trembled with excitement. I sat in the third row of violins and wore my white orchestra jacket like a royal robe.

My heart beat wildly at my first public performance, a school operetta[14]. The auditorium filled to capacity and the audience buzzed while we softly tuned our instruments. Then the spotlight centered on us, and a hush fell as we started to play. I felt sure everyone in the audience was watching me. Daddy and mother smiled proudly at their little girl who held her cherished violin for the whole world to admire.

The years seemed to run more swiftly then. And by the time my sisters graduated, I found myself in the first-violin chair.

Two years later, I graduated. I packed my cherished violin in its case and stepped into the grown-up world. Nurse's training, marriage, working in the hospital, rearing four daughters filled my years.

More years passed. My violin made every move with us, and

道这件事。我知道爸爸和我的祈祷得到了回应。

我拿着琴第一次去学校上课的那天，没有人能够想象我的心情是多么的激动。一连几个月我天天练习，感觉着温暖的木头在我的下巴下，就像我自己身体的延伸。

当我准备好参加学校管弦乐队时，我激动得有些颤抖。我坐在第三排，穿着白色的乐队服装，就像女王的衣服。

参加第一场公共演出，一个学校的轻歌剧，我的心狂乱地跳着。礼堂坐满了人，当我们轻轻地开始演奏乐器时观众中有兴奋的谈话声。然后，灯光集中到了我们这里，当我们正式开始演奏时，全场很肃静。我感到观众席上的每个人都在看着我。爸爸妈妈向那个拿着自己心爱的小提琴，足以让整个世界羡慕的小女儿骄傲地微笑着。

接下来的几年过得很快。到我的姐姐们毕业时，我发现自己坐在了第一排小提琴的椅子上。

两年后，我毕业了。我把心爱的小提琴放进了琴盒中，迈入了成人的世界。护士培训，结婚，在医院工作，抚养4个女儿是我这些年所做的事。

许多年过去了，我的小提琴每次都让我

⑭ **operetta** /ˌɒpəˈretə/ *n.* 轻歌剧

I unpacked-briefly remembering how much I still loved it and promising myself to play it soon.

None of my children cared about the violin. Later, one by one, they married and left home....

Now here I was with the newspaper want ads. I forced my thoughts to the present and read again the ad that had transported me back to childhood memories. Laying aside the paper, I murmured, "I must find my violin."

I discovered the case deep in the recesses[15] of my closet[16]. Opening the lid, I lifted the violin from where it nestled on the rose-velvet lining. My fingers caressed[17] its golden wood. I tuned the strings, miraculously[18] still intact[19], tightened the bow, and put rosin[20] on the dry horsehairs.

And then my violin began to sing again those favorite tunes that had never left my memory. How long I played I'll never know. I thought of Daddy, who did all he could to fill my needs and desires when I was a little girl. I wondered if I had ever thanked him.

At last I laid the violin back in its case. I picked up the newspaper, walked to the phone and dialed the number.

Later in the day, an old car stopped in my driveway. A man in his 30s knocked on the door. "I've been praying someone would answer my ad. My daughter wants a violin so badly," he

们感动，当我们打开它，我把它小心收好时，我记起自己仍然非常喜欢它，并且承诺我自己很快还要用它演奏。

我的孩子没有一个人在乎这把小提琴。之后，一个接一个地接了婚，并离开了家……

现在，在这里我拿着一个报纸上的求购广告。我努力使思绪回到现在，又读了一遍那个使我回到了童年记忆中的广告。把报纸放到一边，我低语到："我一定要找到我的小提琴。"

在储物室中一个隐秘的地方我找到了琴盒。打开盖子，我把放在玫瑰色绒布上的小提琴拿了出来。我用手指轻抚它金色的木头，我拨动琴弦，它们竟然奇迹般地完好无损。紧紧琴弓，然后把松香放在干的马尾毛上。

然后我的小提琴开始再次发出那些我喜欢的而且从未离我记忆而去的旋律。我不知道自己拉了多长时间。我想起了爸爸，当我还是个小女孩的时候，他尽一切所能来满足我的需要和愿望。我想知道自己是否曾经感谢过他。

最后，我把小提琴放回了琴盒。我拿起报纸，走向电话，拨了号码。

这天的晚些时候，一辆老车停在了我的

⑮ **recess** /rɪˈses/ *n.* 壁凹，遥远或隐秘的地方

⑯ **closet** /ˈklɒzɪt/ *n.* （储存物品的）柜橱或小房间

⑰ **caress** /kəˈres/ *v.* 爱抚或抚摸

⑱ **miraculously** /mɪˈrækjʊləslɪ/ *adv.* 奇迹般地，神奇地，不可思议地

⑲ **intact** /ɪnˈtækt/ *adj.* 完整的，无损的

⑳ **rosin** /ˈrɒzɪn/ *n.* 松香

said, examining my instrument. "How much are you asking?"

Any music store, I knew, would offer me a nice sum. But now I heard my voice answer, "Seven dollars."

"Are you sure?" he asked, reminding me so much of Daddy.

"Seven dollars," I repeated, and then added, "I hope your little girl will enjoy it as much as I did."

I closed the door behind him. Peeking out between the drapes, I saw his wife and children waiting in the car. A door suddenly opened and a young girl ran to him as he held out the violin case to her.

She hugged it against her, then dropped to her knees and snapped[21] open the case. She touched the violin lightly as it caught the glow of the late-afternoon sun, then turned and threw her arms around her smiling father.

车道上，一个30多岁的男人敲门。“我一直祈祷有人能回应我的广告，我的女儿太想要一把小提琴了。”他边说边检查着我的乐器。“你要多少钱？”

我知道任何一家音乐店都会给我一笔不小的数目，但是现在我听到我的声音回答“7美元。”

“你确定吗？”他问，使我想起了爸爸。

“7美元”，我重复道，并且又说，“我希望你小女儿像我一样喜欢这把琴。”

他走后我关上门。从窗帘的缝隙中望去，我看到他的妻子和孩子正在车里等着。车门突然开了，一个小女孩跑向他，他把琴盒伸出去给了她。

她紧紧抱着琴盒，然后跪下来打开了它。她轻轻抚摸着小提琴。这时，小提琴吸引了午后太阳的光芒，然后她转身用手臂抱住了她正在微笑的父亲。

㉑ **snap** /snæp/ *v.* 打开

Secrets every achiever knows

每个成功者都知道的秘密

The secret of such commitment is getting past the drudgery and seeing the delight.

如此忘我的秘密在于透过繁重乏味的工作看到光明。

In October 1982, a 25-year-old woman finished the New York City Marathon. No big deal — until you learn that Linda Down has cerebral palsy[1] and was the first woman ever to complete the 26.2-mile race on crutches. Down fell half a dozen times, but kept going until she crossed the finish line, 11 hours after she started. Her handicap limited her speed but not her determination.

Henry Wadsworth Longfellow once wrote: "Great is the art of beginning, but greater the art is of ending." How nice it would be if we all had a genie[2] who could help us finish what we begin. Unfortunately, we don't. But what we do have is a dynamic[3] called discipline — which extracts[4] a high price. Following one of Paderewski's performances, a fan said to him, "I'd give my life to play like that." The brilliant pianist replied, "I did."

Accomplishment is often deceptive because we don't see the pain and perseverance that produced it. So we may credit the achiever with brains, brawn[5] or lucky breaks, and let ourselves off the hook because we fall short in all three. Not that we could all be concert pianists just by exercising enough discipline. Rather, each of us has the makings of success in some endeavor, but we will achieve this only if we apply our wills and work at it.

How can we acquire stick-to-itiveness? There is no simple, fast formula. But I have developed a way of thinking that has rescued my own vacillating[6] will more than once. Here are the basic elements:

1982年10月，一位25岁的女士完成了纽约城马拉松赛。这并不是什么了不起的事，除非你知道林达·唐患有脑性麻痹，并且她是第一位拄着拐杖完成这个26.2里地比赛的女士。尽管摔倒过很多次，但11个小时后她坚持冲过了终点线。她的残疾限制了她的速度，但并没能妨碍她的决心。

朗费罗曾经有一次写过："开始是伟大的艺术，但结束更伟大。"如果我们都有一个神可以帮助我们完成已经开始的事情，那该多好啊。不幸的是，我们没有。但我们却有一种内在的动力叫做自律，这需要付出昂贵的代价。看了Paderewski的一次演出之后，一位崇拜者对他说，"我要用一辈子才能演奏得那么好。"这位才华横溢的钢琴家答道："我正是这么做的。"

成就往往具有欺骗性，因为我们看不到它背后的痛苦与坚忍不拔。我们也许认为有成就的人聪明，身体健壮或运气好，让我们别再自寻烦恼了，因为这三个方面我们都不行。并不是通过足够的训练我们都可以成为钢琴演奏家。我们每个人通过努力都可以在某些方面成功，但必须要有毅力，并且要努力拼搏。

但我总结了一种不止一次把我从犹豫的

❶ **cerebral palsy** 脑性麻痹

❷ **genie** /ˈdʒiːnɪ/ *n.* 神怪，妖怪

❸ **dynamic** /daɪˈnæmɪk/ *n.* 产生变化、行动或影响的力量

❹ **extract** /ɪkˈstrækt/ *v.* 获取，强索

❺ **brawn** /brɔːn/ *n.* 强壮的肌肉；强健的体力

❻ **vacillating** /ˈvæsəleɪtɪŋ/ *adj.* 摇摆不定

"Won't" power. This is as important is willpower. The ancient Chinese philosopher Mencius said, "Men must be decided on what they will not do, and then they are able to act with vigor in what they ought to do."

Discipline means choices. Every time you say yes to a goal or objective, you say not many more. Every prize has its price. The prize is the yes; the price is the no. Igor Gorin, the noted Ukrainian-American baritone[7], told of his early days studying voice. He loved to smoke a pipe, but one day his professor said, "Igor, you will have to make up your mind whether you are going to be a great singer, or a great pipe-smoker, you cannot be both." So the pipe went.

Delayed gratification[8]. M. Scott Peck, M.D., author of the best-seller *The Road Less Traveled*, describes this tool of discipline as "a process of scheduling the pain and pleasure of life in such a way as to enhance the pleasure by meeting and experiencing the pain first and getting it over with."

This might involve routine daily decisions — something as simple as skipping a favorite late-night TV show and getting to bed early, to be wide awake for a meeting the next morning. Or it might involve longer-term resolves. A young widow with three children decided to invest her insurance settlement in a college education for herself. She considered the realities of a tight budget and little free time, but these seemed small sacrifices in return for the doors that a degree would open. Today she is a highly paid

困境中解脱出来的思维模式，以下是基本要点：

“不”的力量。这和意志力同等重要。中国古代的思想家孟子说过：“人必须决定他们不做什么，才能集中精力做好他们应该做的事情。”

自律意味着选择。每次你对某个目标说“是”，你都对其他更多的目标说了“不”。每次成功都有代价。成功是“是”；代价是“不”。Igor Gorin，著名的乌克兰美籍男中音，讲了他开始学唱歌时的经历。他喜欢抽烟，但有一天他的教授说：“Igor，你必须决定你是想成为一名伟大的歌唱家还是一个烟鬼，你不能两个都是。”所以它不再抽烟了。

迟到的喜悦。斯考特·派克是畅销书《捷径》的作者，他这样形容他自律的方法：“这样安排痛苦和欢乐的顺序：通过经历痛苦来提高欢乐并用欢乐战胜痛苦。”

这也许包括日常生活中的决定，比如不看晚间自己喜欢的电视节目，早点儿上床睡觉，以便第二天开会的时候能够保持清醒。或者这可能也需要长期的坚持。一个带着三个孩子的年轻寡妇决定把她的保险投资在自己的大学教育上。她考虑到了财政紧张以及几乎没有业余时间，但这些与学历给他带来

❼ **baritone**
/ˈbærɪtəʊn/
adj. 男中音

❽ **gratification**
/ˌɡrætɪfɪˈkeɪʃn/
n. 喜悦，满意，满足

financial consultant[9].

The secret of such commitment is getting past the drudgery[10] and seeing the delight. "The fact is that many worthwhile endeavors aren't fun," says syndicated radio and TV commentator Mort Crim. "True, all work and no play makes Johnny a dull boy. But trying to turn everything we do into play makes for terrible frustrations, because life — even the most rewarding one — includes circumstances that aren't fun at all. I like my job as a journalist. It's personally satisfying, bit it isn't always fun."

Achieving a balance. Never confuse discipline with rigidity. Perfection is not the aim; rather, strive for the peace of mind that comes from being in charge of yourself.

Most of us need interludes in our work to take a walk or eat snack-whatever revives and refreshes. Your breathers don't need to be lengthy to shake out the cobwebs[11] and give some relief. Such rewards act as incentives[12] for finishing a task, as well as helping you to maintain momentum[13].

True discipline achieves a balance of producing, not driving. Even discipline needs to be disciplined.

Self-development. Disciplined people are happier people because they are fulfilling inner potential. A woman at one of my seminars told me about her six year-old daughter who swam with a team and practiced every morning for an hour, swimming 2000

的机会相比都是小的牺牲。今天她已经成为一位高薪的财务顾问。

如此忘我的秘密在于透过繁重乏味的工作看到光明。“事实是很多有价值的努力都没乐趣，”辛迪加电台和电视台的评论员Mort Crim说，“的确，只工作不玩耍使约翰变成一个大笨蛋，但试着把每件事都变得有意思会带来巨大的失望，因为生活最有价值的一面包括了枯燥乏味。我喜欢我的记者工作，这很令我满意，但并不总是很有乐趣。”

达到平衡。不要把自律和千篇一律混为一谈。完美不是目标；掌握自己，尽力达到心灵上的平静才是目标。

我们每个人工作的时候都需要休息，散散步或吃点东西，做任何可以使我们恢复精力的事情。你休息的时间没必要长得足以把蜘蛛网打扫干净，这样来寻求解脱。这种奖励是对完成工作的激励，同时也帮你保持动力。

真正的自律是达到产出平衡，而不是拼命。甚至自律本身也需要管理。

自我发展。自律的人更快乐，因为他们达到了内心的满足。在我的一个研讨会上，一位女士给我讲了她6岁的女儿的事情，小女孩参加了一个游泳队，每天早晨练习一小

⑨ **consultant**
/kənˈsʌltənt/
n. 顾问

⑩ **drudgery**
/ˈdrʌdʒərɪ/
n. 繁重乏味的工作

⑪ **cobweb**
/ˈkɒbweb/
n. 蜘蛛网

⑫ **incentive**
/ɪnˈsentɪv/
n. 激励，刺激

⑬ **momentum**
/məˈmentəm/
n. 动力，冲力，势头

to 3000 meters, she related a conversation her daughter had with a family friend:

"Do you like swimming? " the friend asked.

"Yes, I love it."

"Is it fun? "

"No! "

That six-year-old had learned what many adults never experience: the joy of discipline and self-development. Unfortunately, the very word discipline puts us off because it sounds restrictive and punitive — like a truant[14] officer stalking[15] us to make sure we *toe the line*[16]. True discipline isn't on your back needling you with imperatives[17]; it is at your side, nudging you with incentives. When you understand that discipline is self-caring, not self-castigating[18], you won't cringe at its mention, but will cultivate it.

Charley Boswell, a former University of Alabama football star with hopes of a professional baseball career, lost his eyesight in World War II, but that didn't stop him "to become the National Blind Golf Champion 17 times. He was quoted as saying, "I never count what I've lost. I only count what I have left." That is self-development — that is discipline.

Habit-changing strategies. Many a person's downfall comes

时，游 2000 至 3000 米，她叙述了女儿和她们家一位朋友的谈话：

“你喜欢游泳吗?”那个朋友问。

“是的，我非常喜欢。”

“它有趣吗?”

“没有!”

那个 6 岁的孩子已经知道了许多大人都未曾体验到的事情：自律和自我发展的快乐。不幸的是，正是自律这个词使我们失去了兴趣，因为它听起来很受限制并且让人难受，好像一个游手好闲的长官偷偷走近我们看我们是否遵守纪律。真正的自律不是用压在身上必须要做的事来烦你；自律就在你身边用激励来提醒你。当你明白自律是对自己的关心而不是自我惩罚，提到它你就不会再害怕，而会注意培养它。

Charley Boswell 从前是阿拉巴马大学的一名足球明星，他希望自己成为职业的棒球运动员，在二战期间失明了，但这并没有阻止他“17 次成为全国盲人高尔夫球赛的冠军。他说：“我从不计较我失去了什么，我只在乎我还有什么。”这就是自我发展，这就是自律。

改变习惯的策略。许多人的败笔在于总想用自己不喜欢的行为来代替坏习惯，从而

⑭ **truant** /ˈtruːənt/

adj. 逃避工作或责任的人，游手好闲的人

⑮ **stalk** /stɔːk/

v. 踱着方步走，偷偷接近

⑯ **toe the line**

服从团体或党的命令，遵从

⑰ **imperative** /ɪmˈperətɪv/

n. 必要的事，必须履行的责任

⑱ **castigate** /ˈkæstɪgeɪt/

n. 严厉责骂、批评或惩罚

in trying to change a bad habit by focusing on an undesirable behavior to replace it.

Countless people tell me they would like to eat better but don't want to "give up" tasty food. Rather than thinking about what they can't have, they should think about what they can eat. Fruit juice with sparkling mineral water is a delicious substitute for high-calorie soft drinks; snacks and cookies prepared with whole grains and fried fruits give candy bars good competition.

It isn't easy to change old habits. An overweight woman came to me during a seminar and said, "I'm so undisciplined. I can't stick to a diet and my house is always a mess. I feel like a slob." I told her she wasn't totally undisciplined. "You made it to this conference. You arrive promptly at each session, and you are neatly dressed." She almost smiled, and then I added, "There's probably a reason why you haven't been able to lose weight or get your home in order."

Later, I found out there was a big reason. She was widowed a year before. Her husband had been an alcoholic who verbally abused her all 24 years of their marriage. It never occurred to her that a poor self-image was keeping her from effecting positive changes. With this realization, she took the next step in bringing more discipline to her life — by going for counseling[19]. Meanwhile, some of her friends offered to come to her house and help her clean up, putting her even more solidly on a habit-changing course.

改变坏习惯。

无以计数的人告诉我，他们想吃得更健康，但又不想放弃美味的食物。他们应该想他们能吃什么，而不是想他们不能吃什么。果汁加矿泉汽水是高热量的软饮料很好的替代品；全麦的零食小点心和炸水果也不比巧克力差。

改变老习惯并不容易。一个研讨会上，一位超重的女士走过来对我说："我一点都不自律。我不能坚持控制饮食，我的房间也总是一团糟。我像是一个不修边幅的人。"我告诉她，她并不是完全不能自律。"你参加了这次会议，每个阶段你都及时到场，而且你衣着整齐。"她几乎笑了，然后我又说："你减肥不成功或没能把房间整理好，也许有其他的原因。"

之后，我发现一个很大的原因：她一年前成了寡妇。她丈夫曾是个酒鬼，他们结婚的24年他总是骂她。她从没想到过是一个不好的自我印象影响了她积极有效地改变现状。意识到这一点之后，她采取了下一步措施使自己生活更有规律，通过寻求专业意见。同时，她的一些朋友也主动提出到她家帮助她打扫房间，这使她更坚定地走上了改变习惯的道路。

⑲ **counseling** /ˈkaʊnsəlɪŋ/ *n.* 专业指导

Mind over matter. I remember my school days and Mom's regular reveille[20]: "Time to get up!" I agonized[21] in bed until the last minute and ran my mother's patience short. Then I went away to college and had to get myself up. Finally, tired of waging war with waking, I decided that when the alarm rang, I would rise — just because I wanted to, regardless of how I felt. It has worked ever since.

In Feeling Good, *The New Mood Therapy*, David D. Burns, M.D., writes: "Motivation does not come first, action does! You have to prime the pump. If you wait until you're 'in the mood,' you may wait forever." When you don't feel like doing something, you tend to put it off, but it's often after we get involved in a task that we become highly motivated.

Discipline is habit-forming. A little leads to more, because the benefits prove increasingly desirable. When you finally overcome inertia[22], you will feel better all around. We are at our best — physically and mentally — when we are disciplined.

*集中注意力于要解决的事情。*我记得上学时妈妈每天都喊："该起床了！"我痛苦地躺在床上直到不得不起来，而且也把妈妈惹得不耐烦了。后来我离开家去上大学，必须天天自己起床。最后，厌烦了与起床做斗争，我决定闹钟一响我就起床，只是因为我想这么做，不管感受如何。从那时以后我一直这么做。

在 *Feeling Good, The New Mood Therapy* 一书中大卫·伯恩斯写道："不是先有动机，而是先有行动！你要先给水泵注水使之启动起来。如果你要等到你心情好，你可能要一直等下去。"当你不想做什么的时候，你可能会先把它放下，但通常是你开始做这件事之后你的动力才会更足。

自律是一个习惯养成的过程。由一点到更多，因为好处越来越让人向往。当你最终克服惯性，你会感觉更好。当我们自律时，我们的身体和精神都会处于最佳状态。

⑳ **reveille**
/rɪˈvælɪ/
n. 起床号、鼓等

㉑ **agonized**
/ˈæɡənaɪzd/
adj. 表示痛苦的

㉒ **inertia**
/ɪˈnɜːʃə/
n. 惰性，惯性

图书在版编目（CIP）数据

英汉对照·心灵阅读．4，励志篇/王亚男编译．—北京：外文出版社，2004
ISBN 7－119－03745－5

Ⅰ．英…　Ⅱ．王…　Ⅲ．英语－对照读物，英、汉　Ⅳ．H319．4

中国版本图书馆 CIP 数据核字（2004）第 058989 号

外文出版社网址：
http://www.flp.com.cn
外文出版社电子信箱：
info@flp.com.cn
sales@flp.com.cn

英汉对照·心灵阅读（四）
励志篇
编　译　王亚男
审　校　林　立

责任编辑　王　蕊　相　永
封面设计　时振晓
印刷监制　张国祥
出版发行　外文出版社
社　址　北京市百万庄大街 24 号　邮政编码　100037
电　话　（010）68995963/6075（编辑部）
（010）68329514/68327211（推广发行部）
印　刷　北京顺义振华印刷厂
经　销　新华书店/外文书店
开　本　大 32 开　字　数　150 千字
印　数　00001－10000 册　印　张　8.875
版　次　2004 年 7 月第 1 版第 1 次印刷
装　别　平
书　号　ISBN 7－119－03745－5/H·1629（外）
定　价　15.80 元